THE MEMOIRS OF JULIAN HAWTHORNE

THE MACMILLAN COMPANY
NEW YORK · BOSTON · CHICAGO · DALLAS
ATLANTA · SAN FRANCISCO

MACMILLAN & CO., Limited
LONDON · BOMBAY · CALCUTTA
MELBOURNE

**THE MACMILLAN COMPANY
OF CANADA, Limited**
TORONTO

JULIAN HAWTHORNE
at eighty-one years of age

THE MEMOIRS

OF

Julian Hawthorne

EDITED BY HIS WIFE

EDITH GARRIGUES HAWTHORNE

1938

THE MACMILLAN COMPANY

NEW YORK

B
H 3988

For permission given to Mr. Hawthorne to quote in these reminiscences certain excerpts from his book, "Nathaniel Hawthorne and His Wife," published fifty-three years ago, I wish to thank the publishers, the Houghton Mifflin Company, holders of the original copyright.

As Mr. Hawthorne touched on some of the events and personalities appearing in these "Memoirs," during his seventeen years as weekly contributor to the "Book Page" of the *Pasadena Star News,* I wish to express my grateful appreciation to its Editor, Chas. H. Prisk, for a most valued association.

E. G. H.

FOREWORD

The Memoirs of Julian Hawthorne are the annals of his friendships with many of the world's famous men and women during his long and productive life, as author, journalist, and poet.

His first novel "Bressant" was published in 1873, and more than fifty volumes followed from his pen, during the years: among them "A Fool of Nature" for which he was awarded the *New York Herald* Novel-contest prize, of $10,000. Julian Hawthorne spent many years in England, and in 1928 his English reminiscences appeared, in "Shapes That Pass."

In the present volume, he has given us his American Memoirs, which were completed toward the end of his life; but time was not allotted him to undertake the task of giving them their final consideration, for that finesse, order and, as near as possible, that literary perfection, the accomplishment of which is the very core of life for an author.

In editing these American Memoirs of Julian Hawthorne I have undertaken this final process of filing off edges that were left in the rough, when Death stayed his hand. In doing so I have relived the friendships and scenes which his constant and delightful narration made vitally real to me.

It has been a work happily entered into, and consecrated to a deep and loving memory of my husband, Julian Hawthorne.

Edith Garrigues Hawthorne

CONTENTS

Contents

Contents

PART ONE

Family Matters—The Author as
a Small Boy

On Writing
an Autobiography

I HAVE been occupied with biographical and even autobiographical matters, with the reminiscences of fellow wayfarers, and have felt the importance of the unimportant: not analysis of Emerson's "Sphinx," but the squeaking of his boots during one of his lectures; not his soul, but his clay; not that Thoreau built a hut beside Walden, but that he lost his temper when the Selectmen put him into Concord jail. And because I was an unconsidered urchin instead of a Peer of the Realm, I was admitted to sights and contacts withheld from the elect.

But the urchin remembered what he saw, and lived long enough to understand its value for the succeeding era, which had been fed up and to spare with the heroic sort of thing. So, although academic historians may find small value in my reminiscences, archeologists will grin over the mouldering pages: "So, the Concord Group were human after all!" Not that I am a scandalmonger, but that I was not yet conscious of artificial values and, like Mark Antony, spoke right on and told you that which you yourselves do know,—of yourselves, and were comforted to learn that the high and mighty were just plain folk at bottom. For my part, I supposed that all the world was composed of Emersons, Alcotts and Margaret Fullers, and had no suspicions of my singular advantages. It takes time and experience to learn the preciousness of ignorance.

Goethe attempted his autobiography, but subsequent analysis of his career showed that he leaned to *Dichtung* rather than *Wahrheit*. Shakespeare wrote no autobiography, unless we take all his plays, poems and sonnets to be that. Benvenuto Cellini, in a famous volume, told his adventures and achievements, but of the man behind them we learn little. Montaigne wrote his Essays, taking half a lifetime to do it, but inadvertently side-steps himself. Had Samuel Johnson's biography been an autobiography, it would have been perfect: but there you are! The others failed either for the same reason that a man puts on a coat and trousers in public, or because they didn't know how.

My inference, strengthened by my personal experience, is that the thing can't be done. I can tell no end of anecdotes about my contemporaries, and I am by no means apt to think of myself as a rare and indispensable person; and yet I know that, if I could put my real self on paper, the story would have value and interest.

I should like, in these memoirs, to give you a warm and live picture of New England existence in my time, and of my own impulses, emotions and reactions in that environment. Of the former, something may be possible, though it is difficult to divine just what you would care to know, and what is pithless and penumbral. But from the other—something stronger than my own desire withholds me. There is a decree of the High Gods that forbids it: I must be content with my anecdotes. There is a limit of disclosure beyond which mortals mustn't go, or civilization would blow up. We may lead one another so far into our labyrinth; to go further would betray—not merely our insignificant selves but human nature: because in those unsounded depths we are all one, and mystically bound to keep the faith. The Minotaur, in the old classic fable, lurks in the center of the labyrinth and devours impiety.

Also life is not essentially funny, and even funny things have a serious side. But it pays a story-teller to be amusing; a G. B. S. makes money and wins popularity. Turn your amusing side to your audience, or, in self-defense, they will turn your tragedy into a joke. Wit, humor, irony are the arrows that hit the goal; cheaply come by, but they ring the bell. I could have made little Dio Lewis a pathetic figure without diverging from facts. But I sagaciously chose his diverting aspects; and got closer even to Emerson by the path of smiles; his serious side has become commonplace.

Men nowadays—women, too, perhaps—get together and swap stories, and nine times out of ten break up with a laugh. Ella Wheeler—before she added the Wilcox—sang her true song:

> Laugh, and the world laughs with you;
> Weep, and you weep alone:
> For this brave old earth must borrow its mirth,
> But has trouble enough of its own.

Good doctrines, not cynical. And if I were a publisher, I would bank on Mark Twain rather than Dante.

Nathaniel Hawthorne
as a Companion

MY FATHER, in his boyhood, was a cheerful and sociable fellow, rather prone to dominate his companions, thanks to his superior wit and muscle. In college he was rather a leader than led, and on the whole didn't take life too seriously. He was healthy, vigorous and adventurous, and might have followed an ancestral bias toward the sea; but that would have left his family unprotected. He was a great reader of all accessible books; he followed the line of least resistance, sat at home, and read, and walked to the seashore; held aloof from Salem society, whose primness and religiosity he found antipathetic; and being imaginative, did a little scribbling, in verse or prose. This propensity grew upon him, doubtless stimulated by his sister Elizabeth. Why not, after all, be a writer? His ancestors might scoff at him; but it was as honorable a profession as any.

At intervals, he might break loose and forgather with a friend or two—Bridge, Pierce, or another; or explore, on foot or by stagecoach, neighborhoods not too remote, making mental notes all the while, for possible stories, but not as yet quite seriously. He didn't drink, or care for tobacco; on the whole he preferred looking on to joining in, and could exercise a gift of silence—

6

which Emerson noted long afterward: "Hawthorne rides well his horse of the night!" Emerson uttered an Emersonianism every time he opened his mouth.

Hawthorne's dark-browed look seemed more hospitable than responsive, and made him desirable company, though likely to make the epigrammatist doubt himself. Hawthorne, when driven to utterance—as sometimes in an after-dinner speech at an English dinnertable—would twitch his shoulders and let fly something brief and poignant, hitting the goal. Your first reaction would be to laugh at the wit, and then the penetration would sober you; as fencers, at the first contact of the foils, recognize a master. At the Boston Saturday Club meetings, Hawthorne, though always desired, seldom attended; but brought with him a good appetite, as the elder Henry James once remarked with a chuckle.

On the other hand, when the stevedores at the wharf ventured to slacken on their jobs, the taciturn overseer unexpectedly thundered and lightninged at them, so that they jumped in dismay, recognizing that he was the son of a mariner who, legend said, was the "sternest man who ever trod a deck." On the other hand Hawthorne admits, in his preface to "Twice Told Tales," that "whether from lack of power, or an unconquerable reserve, the author's touches have often an effect of tameness"; and it may be admitted that once in a while the tone is almost feminine. In fact, inasmuch as he uniformly used a pen-name in the early days, you might fancy that the author was a woman. But anon the deep male note breaks through, and you guess again.

Sophia Peabody—Birth of
Julian Hawthorne

NEARLY four years passed between the first meeting of Nathaniel Hawthorne and Sophia Peabody and their marriage, though both realized a mutual love at first sight. Mrs. Hawthorne, in telling her children, many years afterwards, of these first meetings with their father, used to say that his presence from the very beginning exercised so strong a magnetic attraction upon her that, instinctively and in self-defense, as it were, she drew back and repelled him. The power which she felt in him alarmed her; she did not understand what it meant, and was only able to feel that she must resist it.

By degrees, however, her resistance was overcome; and in the end she realized that they had loved each other at first sight. Her long illness and her consequent resolve never to marry were back of this reticence and quasi-fear. In a letter to her sister Elizabeth Peabody she wrote: "My long apprenticeship to physical unrest has not made me love mortal life for itself. You mistake my state of mind about this. The reason that I am not impatient to die is because I have gained courage to live here as long as God wills. It is a feeling of mingled content with His will. I should think it weak and distrustful of His tenderness to wish to be in any other situation than just that in which I am.

"After using all human means to be in the best condition of health, I am utterly content if they fail. I have no regrets as far as myself is concerned. I am happy because, first, my heart, and, daily, more and more my reason assure me that there is a God. This one absolute truth is quite enough for me. It is the central light of the Universe; now that I have fixed my eye upon it, I am absolutely happy, and cheerful. Nothing can make me despond."

In speaking of her coming marriage with Nathaniel Hawthorne, in a letter to her friend Miss Foote, Sophia writes: "I marvel how I can be so blessed among mortals, now that the very king and poet of the world shall be my eternal companion henceforth. It fills me with an awful beatitude—and I worship God with trembling love; but I am not afraid. Time is so swallowed up in Eternity now that I have found my being in him, that life seems all one. Now and the remotest hereafter are blended together. In the presence of majestic, serene nature we shall stand transfigured with a noble, complete happiness. This most bountiful month, so rich in treasures of verdure and fullness, will find us bound by earthly as we long have been by heavenly ties. The ceremony is nothing—our true marriage was three years ago."

And so on July 9, 1842, the marriage took place at the house of Dr. Peabody, No. 13 West Street, Boston. The future that lay before the married lovers had in it its full share of sadness, of joy, of honor and achievement, but the chapter of their courtship had a rare bloom of loveliness, which can come but once even to the pure in heart.

9

Thus, in due course of time, after my sister Una had arrived to crown their happiness, I was born; and had the angels commissioned to such duties asked me before my arrival under what conditions I should prefer the event to take place, I would have replied without hesitation, "Let me be the only son of Nathaniel Hawthorne and his wife Sophia, born in Boston, Massachusetts, at 1 o'clock in the morning of June 22nd, in the year 1846." That at any rate was what happened, and therefore, boy and man, I have lived contented for now these five and eighty years, and the beams of my setting sun seem full as warm as those of its arising.

I was especially sagacious in selecting Boston and its neighborhood for my birth-scene; because not only had Oliver Wendell Holmes declared it to be the Hub of the Universe, but so many good people were already there. Ralph Waldo Emerson, for instance, after finding himself incompatible with a more or less orthodox pulpit in Boston, withdrew to the pine-woods of Concord, indited his defiance to the world, and was happy and famous ever after.

Concord is only twenty miles from Boston. The atmosphere soon became transcendental, alluring but heady, and many gentle inebriates congregated there. Thoreau actually was born there, and there he died, after holding out for forty years. Alcott, introduced by Plato, and fostered by Emerson, arrived there in what would have been his youth had he ever been other than antique.

Ellery Channing, related to the great William Ellery, the Unitarian, and himself a sort of semi-dumb poet, rebel and philosopher, finally settled there and persisted to a great age. Hawthorne came last of all, but departed

with the least possible suffering. My grandmother was helped in her offices by my Aunt Lizzie Peabody, who was one of the most learned and beneficent women of her time. So the baby's auspices were most favorable.

My father was employed meanwhile in the Salem Customhouse; and when my great adventure was over, we all settled down in our Salem dwelling. As you already know, my sister Una had arrived two years before I did, and five years later Rose was to join us; but her nativity was in the Berkshire Hills, at the other end of the state. Further additions would have been an anticlimax; so we stopped there.

All this time, I had known nothing of Concord, for the Old Manse there had been only the honeymoon home of our parents, while Una alone was in time to share it with them. I was city-bred, though the hills and the sea would have been more to my taste. Boston is a seaport; so is Salem; but access to the shore was less easy than it probably is now; and Concord lies in a gentle valley a score of miles inland—by the old road which the British soldiers traversed, just before returning at the double-quick, after experiencing the effects of that "shot heard round the world," which Emerson mentions in his poem. The little episode put Concord on the map, and in history, a long generation before Emerson and the others of his conclave hove in sight; I think it was not until the sages had been well established that the sons and grandsons of the sires that conquered at the Bridge suspected that Transcendentalism was of practical value to the valiant little village. The newcomers—all except Thoreau, who, after all, was a native—paid their taxes and discussed the Spirit, which, at worst, might be jolly but not requiring discipline by the Selectmen. After yanking Thoreau out of his Walden hut and locking him up in Concord jail, they let the Movement alone. But I shall return to Thoreau further along.

Concord, as I was saying, lies twenty miles inland from Boston, and was insalubrious for Hawthorne, whose blood was tinted with the dark blue of the Seven Seas sailed by his ancestors for many a generation. But the Fitchburg Railroad had a branch between Concord and Boston and the tickets cost but sixty cents; so that the author, at this moderate extravagance, could journey to the Old Corner Bookstore at Washington and School streets and there forgather with Ticknor and Fields, his publishers and friends, and with other friends trying, like himself, to make a living with their quills.

If he seldom improved this advantage, we may ascribe it to the artistic temperament, or what you will. Having hung up his pilgrim's hat and staff in "The Wayside," as he named our house, he liked to stay there, content with the society of his wife and children.

As for the climate of Concord, it had a range of between 112 degrees above zero and 20 below; but these were extremes; it was commonly satisfied with from 80 to 90 above and zero down; and we had swimming, skating and sleighing, in their proper seasons. Hawthorne didn't complain; he had a to-and-fro path along the top of his hillside and was now at an age when looking out from his study windows at snowdrifts might be more agreeable than ploughing through them, as in his youth. He relinquished such hardy sports to his offspring, who were just in tune for them. But in those last years he doubtless thought a good deal about "Our Old

Home," as he called it—and the book of essays from his English Journals was the last volume published in his lifetime. There is something felicitous in the fact that his last romance, which saw the light only when his life was over, is a romance of immortality. There is a sadness in the idea which prompts the story. It is the dead alone who can gain by immortality. For the living there must be the certainty of death, or life itself would become unnatural and vain. Hawthorne endeavored to express how terribly sad would be its indefinite continuance. But, dissatisfied, he laid "Septimius" aside and substituted "The Dolliver Romance," which deals with the same thought. But the story was never to see an end. Worn by illness and anxiety Hawthorne laid down his pen, and

> The unfinished window in Aladdin's tower
> Unfinished must remain!

I have been writing ahead of my narrative, which begins (to my consciousness) about the epoch of the composition of "The Scarlet Letter." That was in Salem, in 1849–50, when Una and I were six and four years old respectively; she being my guide and ruler, and I her willing and sedulous ape.

Hawthorne's brows were dark, but beneath their shadow was a light unquenchable. We had our playthings, no superfluity, and with our father as playmate we needed none. Moreover, his hands were large, supple and with square-topped fingers; he could manufacture readily a manikin, a house, or a boat, and paint comic faces to grin unawares on the underside of lids and covers. A man of magic, creating the impression that, in his most wonderful achievements, he never half tried. "My magic," was his sufficient explanation, when some-

14

thing inexplicable occurred in the household—with a lift of the right eyebrow, implying, "That was easy!"

As to teaching in the serious sense, he left all that to our mother and our Aunt Elizabeth Peabody, who was abundantly competent; and when in doubt on any subject he would appeal to her superior wisdom and delight in following her law: "Mamma . . . What? . . . Where? . . . How?" And to her he was the wisest of mankind; it was lovely to see them together, implanting in us thus early reverence for the home ties. Such seed stays intact through all vicissitudes.

There was little touching religion in such conversation as we overheard, or in his writings. But our mother was a spontaneous incarnation of religious faith, as we have seen in her letter to her sister regarding her will to live despite her constant illness. In the "Twice Told Tales" there are religious references now and then, the reactions of the mind of a young man who accepted God without argument; and in "The Marble Faun" are comments on the Roman Catholic dogma, but rather as of an artist contemplating human life than as a seeker for guidance. My father became acquainted at different times with several Swedenborgians—in his early days with William Pike, and afterwards with Powers, the sculptor, and with Dr. J. J. Garth Wilkinson in London; and he remarked in one of his journals that he had always found something remarkable in men of the faith.

In England, in the 1850's, it was the custom to open the day with prayer, in which the whole household joined. It was deemed incumbent upon us, therefore, as the family of the American Consul, when we were in Liverpool, to maintain a religious attitude; so our father bought the Book of Common Prayer, and read aloud each morning to the assembled family and servants. Extraordinary, for a "shy" man, and yet characteristic. He would tackle whatever job came to him, as a matter of course.

Hawthorne, in "The Blithedale Romance," mentions overhearing, unwillingly, his friend Hollingsworth's "awful privacy with his Creator," on his knees in the next bedroom. But he never discussed religion in set terms either in his writings or in talk. He "believed" in God, but never sought to define him. In his boyhood he had read "The Fathers of the Early Christian Church," and had, willy-nilly, sat occasionally under strenuous pulpiteers; and in the character Dimmesdale, in "The Scarlet Letter" he recognizes the power of religious appeal. He deeply accepted his wife's rejoicing faith, and perceived the limitations of reason. Our mother upon occasions expressed her faith and reverence in speech; our father in caverns submarine and unsounded, yet somehow apparent; he had that faculty of speech without utterance which is said to have belonged to the most ancient peoples. Thought and emotion might be discerned in his eyes, if you had eyes to penetrate them; but usually you could see only sunny plains and sierras which suggested merely a prevalent state of mind.

But he loved mystery as the depths of the midnight sky which the wisdom of mortality cannot penetrate. It was the symbol of the holiness of the spirit, made for worship, not knowledge. Accordingly, we children grew up in reverence, without attempt at understanding enigmas such as the Immaculate Conception. The meaning was that real things cannot be spoken; divine philosophy being not dull and crabbed but musical as Apollo's lute. This is my interpretation of our daily intercourse at the Wayside and elsewhere. So sermons heard in pews were what an Oxford senior wrangler would have pronounced supererogatory.

Nathaniel Hawthorne
and His Children

MY FATHER read aloud to us children Spenser's "Faerie Queene." I beheld the knights in their shining armor, their crested helmets, their lances and excaliburs, and pined to be one of them. "Be faithful, brave and true in deed and word!" was the obligation of knighthood. My mother, perceiving the moral advantage of knighthood, and the stimulus afforded to the inward by the outward boy, promptly fitted me with a helmet, on the crest of which blazed the Dragon of the great Pendragon-ship with wings outspread; and a glorious tail streaming behind it was made of cardboard covered with silver paper. In the sunshine in our back garden my aspect, prancing to and fro, was glorious; and my father contributed a real sword of tempered steel with a gilded hilt and a scabbard of black leather. Meanwhile I took riding lessons (though not in armor), and the corporal and the major made me an all-round swordsman. I must have been quite a formidable little tyke, and the chivalrous manners of knighthood were in keeping. No doubt Edmund Spenser would have been gratified.

17

Tennyson's "Knights of the Round Table" came later; the creed of his knights was graven on my memory, and I afterward made an illumination of them on a sheet of vellum, and presented them to my mother.

Like Ulysses, we are part of all that we have met; and the memory of the things that we have known, including the opinions we have formed of them, passes before us toward the end of the journey, not in chronological order (not by intention, but haphazard), the things of today arm in arm with those of childhood or of age, and thereby sometimes gaining new significances.

Memory is a queer creature, hard to keep within the confines of sequence. I have been credited with unusual powers to recall things past, because I remember persons and events of seventy and eighty years ago. The explanation is that in childhood and youth contacts with environment are fresh, and so imprint themselves distinctly. Afterward, novelties are rarer, and impressions become less legible, curiosity no longer sharpens attention, unless its subject is unprecedented; even now, for example, I would not forget a new Donati comet, like that of 1858; or the discovery of a complete copy of Sappho's lost lyrics. But the faces of persons recently met, and still more their names, soon fade out, as in the haps and mishaps of current existence the individual loses itself in the type.

But the tricks of memory and forgetting are numberless. When I applied for matriculation at Harvard in 1863, fate assigned me to Professor Sophocles; fierce black eyes, tumultuous and abundant hair and beard, snow-white; except for the fierceness, he much resembled the marble statue of his name in the Vatican Gallery in Rome. "Vot is your name?" he asked. I stammered and hesitated, stumbling among inchoate fragments of Greek history of two or three thousand years ago. But the professor was impatient and irascible. "Do you gome to Harvard to be daught your name?" His voice was as the thunder of Homer's Polusphlosboio Thalasses. I forgot the name, but have the episode.

Another thing in this connection: Suppose I happen to recall, inadvertently, some isolated person or occurrence of the past. As I contemplate it, it ceases to be isolated, and throws out a hundred octopus-feelers which seize upon surrounding matters until, surprisingly, I become aware once more of whatever is pertinent to the occasion. So, on the whole, don't be surprised at whatever these pages may tell or omit. Like the man at the dance-hall piano, I am doing my best.

As a boy at school, my father learned his lessons easily, but was averse to schooling, and was irregular, and was similarly independent at college; I don't think he anticipated scholarship for me, but he wanted me to have the contacts. He died in my freshman year. My mother afterward told me that he had been content with my fortune thus far, but no doubt he would have wished me at least to take a degree. But my voice was all for war, and in the last months of his life he did not forbid my enlistment. He had always stimulated my patriotism with his tales of our Revolution, so that I thirsted for the blood of Englishmen, though I much liked those I happened to know. In our Civil War, I transferred my British animosities to the Southerners; but they fortunately escaped my wrath by the Peace of Appomattox. Besides, I had become the head of the family, and mustn't leave them unprotected.

Family Life

NATHANIEL HAWTHORNE was averse to fine raiment, though in England he was obliged by the dignity of his office to keep sufficiently supplied with black broadcloth. At the Wayside a humble sack coat sufficed him, and for Boston he would put on a talma (as it was called), an overall garment halfway between a long loose topcoat and a cape, of a fashion handed down from old times, affected by middle-aged gentlemen; Fields had one like it. It was becoming and suggested the title of "Field Marshal Hawthorne" that Fields had given him. In fact it was made of fine imported English material, and my father had worn it in the years before his marriage.

After my father's death, my mother had the stuff made over into an up-to-date Prince Albert coat for me, which for ten years was my best garment. In color it was a very dark navy blue. I recall as vividly one other coat; when a small lad I made daily journeys to the village post office for letters, dressed in a little scarlet coat embroidered with black braid, and with my hair, curled on a stick, against my will, hanging down my back, to the derision of the mannerless little Irish boys along the way, and the loud barking of the big black dog which aided and abetted them.

One event is conspicuous, as I look back to those childhood days through the vista of years, exciting my curiosity ever since, but unrevealed till now. I was walking home from the post office with my mail bag, and was passing the long white picket-fence between Farmer Moore's pasture and the road. I was musing on the vicissitudes of mortal life, and rattling my little stick along the pickets; and I was saying to myself, "I am seven years old, and I may live to be seventy; but I know that I shall never know more than I do now."

That was my sober conviction then; and as the decades go by I am more and more disposed to think that I was somehow right. Apart from hearsay and mere information, how much does anybody know? We may even forget the burden of those voices in the air which our childhood heard, conveying the only wisdom which lives and lasts—

> The cloud-capped towers, the gorgeous palaces,
> The solemn temples, the great globe itself,
> Yea, all which it inherits, shall dissolve,
> Leave not a rack behind.

I quote from memory; but you get the idea?

Vividly I recall early days when Una and I and our elders dwelt in an old house on Mall Street, Salem, around 1849–50. It was, I think, part of some local real estate belonging to the Mannings, our paternal grandmother's people. On the ground floor was a large kitchen, where, in cold weather, informal visitors would sometimes come to sit before the huge old fireplace. Above this was the parlor, and over that the guest-chamber, a place to us children at once intimidating and inviting—for its aspect was severe and formal, which repelled us; and Grandmother Hawthorne was dying there, which tempted us with a lure of the unknown and unimaginable. We knew that souls of the dead went to heaven—how was the transference effected? There was something religious about it; it must be reverenced, and we were bred to reverence. But we were also born to curiosity, and that is indelible.

How did it happen that our grandmother lay dying in our house? Until he married, Nathaniel Hawthorne had lived all his life in the Union Street house—except the years when he attended Bowdoin College. With him lived his mother (born Elizabeth Manning, and a beauty in her time) and his two sisters, Elizabeth and Louisa. Upon his marriage he naturally removed elsewhere, and first to the Old Manse in Concord, for a four-year honeymoon: and mother and sisters remained as before. But other changes now took place: Louisa, the only social-minded one of the group, went forth on a visiting tour, while the two Elizabeths, mother and daughter, always even stricter recluses than Nathaniel had been, stayed on in a dual solitude.

In fact, Mrs. Hawthorne, now approaching her eightieth year, had shut herself in her chamber twoscore years before, on receiving news of her husband's death of yellow fever in Surinam. It was a Salem custom for widows to seclude themselves for a season, but never before to this extreme. Now, after her son's departure, she fell ill, and the illness was deemed serious. Her daughter Elizabeth was incapable of giving her adequate care, and the only recourse was to transfer the venerable lady to us on Mall Street, where our own

22

mother could bestow skilled attention and love into the bargain.

"The Scarlet Letter"

THE glimpses which my sister Una and I had of our grandmother Hawthorne, when she came to us in her final illness, made a solemn impression. We saw a tall, dignified figure, with a countenance like our father's—his powerful brows and deep dark eyes. The occasion must have been momentous to her also—her first emergence into the world after that long seclusion. She was of a noble but very sensitive nature; a strange temperament, deepened but not embittered by her self-imposed solitary confinement. Her dignity veiled timidity and shyness; after her lifetime of widowhood she was almost virginal once more. Now, her strength failing, and her eyes beholding a vision of reunion with her Beloved, she was come to us for security and peace. She lay on the great antique bed in the hushed and shadowy chamber, silent, facing the Mystery, dimly conscious perhaps of the enveloping love and tenderness of our mother's ministrations.

And meanwhile, in his little attic study overhead, sat our father composing his Romance, yet attentive to what passed below, and careful to subdue sounds inevitable in children's lives. No wonder if a shadow rests upon the pages of "The Scarlet Letter," and if there is a depth in the story deeper than even its tragic theme might account for.

At intervals, meanwhile, the author had jotted down

23

in his notebook comments on the actual passing scene. The insight and pathos of them are touched with a sad humor. Some of them were afterward transcribed for publication by his widow; but for a reason, I will adduce passages from them once more.

The outstanding personage in the story of "The Scarlet Letter" is not Hester Prynne, nor her lover Dimmesdale, nor the avenger Roger Chillingworth. All these are, in their several ways and degrees, guilty of the committed sin. But among this group stands one who is innocent—the infant, the little girl—the daughter of the lovers, Pearl.

Such a figure is almost inevitable in a tale of passion. But the conventional novelist finds difficulty in handling it; it must be pathetic, but pathos may become wearisome; or it may be a sinister influence in the tale, which leads to melodrama. So it is usually dismissed with mere regretful mention, and that, too, is unsatisfactory. It becomes expedient, therefore, to portray it less in itself than in its embarrassing effect upon its parents; a menace, a shadow, in the background, not concrete and salient before the footlights. In short, the poor, dim waif is hardly less an annoyance in print than it would be in the flesh.

But Hawthorne escapes the dilemma by yielding to Pearl the leading rôle in the drama. In the beginning, the mere fact of her existence had betrayed the lovers' secret; thenceforward, from an involuntary agent, she becomes predominant. She manifests a will and soul of her own, scorns social rebuffs; says, "I am!—who gainsays my right to be?" Thus, in her, the illegitimate declare legitimacy, and we, not they, are in peril.

When eighty-five years ago, Hawthorne composed his story, it was early in the day for such doctrine. Though more radical than many claiming the title, he would not pose as reformer; but if truth lay in his path, he would not sidestep it. Pearl, in her own view, was right, and all others wrong; she would have scorned vindication. We see her seize the reins; and beside her assured vitality, the other figures on the stage appear inert and pale. She is no extravaganza of fancy, but the pith and support of the story; the only statutes she conforms to are her own. To her own mother, of whose impassioned surrender she is the consequence, she appears an appalling enigma; to Hawthorne, directing upon her his penetrating and reverent gaze—because reverent the more penetrating—she becomes Reality, not to be tampered with. With the other, the conventional figures, he might permit himself some craftsman liberties, but not with Pearl! Where could he find a prototype for her? Perhaps nearer home than he himself at the moment suspected.

The mystery of unspoiled childhood is rooted deep in us all; it reaches past the individual to the remotest past—to the endless variety underlying personality. None can tell what may emerge from that depth; in one it may be evil; in another, the genius of a Sappho or a Caesar. Any ancestral vice or virtue may lurk beneath infantile innocence, to be fostered, or obliterated, by the chances of the future.

Where should Hawthorne look for a prototype for Pearl, that innocent consequence of Hester's surrender to Dimmesdale?

Una, his first-born, had inherited much of her father's nature, though not of the faculty to express itself in art.

25

And it happened that the child's reactions to the scene in the guest-chamber, where her grandmother's life was ebbing away, shed new light upon her character.

Two children could hardly differ from each other more than did Hawthorne's daughter Una from Pearl, the child of his imagination. But he, adventuring into the inner chambers of Being, might discover there interweaving threads which the future might unite. As John Wesley said of the drunkard, "There, but for the grace of God, go I." Heredity is beyond mortal fathoming.

Of Pearl, Hawthorne says: "Man had marked her mother by a Scarlet Letter, alienating her from human sympathy. God, as a direct consequence of the sin, had given her a lovely child, connecting her forever with mortals. But Hester discerned in her a depth of hue which lacked reference and adaptation to the world. Her elements, though beautiful and brilliant, were in disorder—or with an order peculiar to themselves. The mother's impassioned existence had transmitted to the unborn infant the rays of its mortal life—the crimson stains, the fiery luster, the black shadow, the untempered light—the whole warfare of the mother's spirit—her wild, defiant mood—were perpetuated in Pearl. In her fancy it might be illuminated by the morning radiance of a child's dispositon; but, hereafter, become perhaps prolific of storm and whirlwind.

"And sometimes, so intelligent, yet inexplicable, would be the child's look—so perverse, almost malicious, and always accompanied by a wild flow of spirits, that Hester could almost believe her, not a human child, but fantastic sprite, which would presently fly away with a mocking smile. In their home, her mood, ever creative,

26

would impart itself to a thousand objects as a torch kindles flame wherever applied. But, singularly, she created never a friend, but sowed broadcast the Dragon's Teeth, against which she rushed to battle—as recognizing an adverse world, and training fierce energies to make good her cause against it."

Pearl is never depicted as, in herself, hateful, but only as brimming over with lawless impulse, which may have a beauty of its own. She has no regrets, no compunctions; a sinless infant, she is yet Sin's very self walking the earth in her own right. As such, in dark moments, she is seen by her own mother; more terrible than the scarlet symbol fixed on Hester's garment, the roots of Pearl are in her soul. And we might infer from Hawthorne's analysis that, could evil instead of good be the law of human beings, we might behold, underlying the awful scenery of hell, a diabolic splendor and delight.

Abstract musings could hardly evolve a portrait so undeniable as this. As the author afterward admits, "I was suffering at the time from a great diversity and severity of emotion." And Goethe remarks, "Who ne'er his bread in sorrow ate, he knows ye not, ye Heavenly powers!" But where did the creator of Pearl find his model?

"The Scarlet Letter" was composed, for the most part, during the torrid heat of a New England summer. The narrow house, and the yard outside, must serve as a playground for the two children: only that secluded guest-chamber wherein Hawthorne's mother lay dying, was denied them. The writer must sit with his study door open, to overhear and, at the need, moderate their involuntary exclamations—a bright, incongruous embroidery upon that somber background. All children are dramatists, and must build their "make-believe" out of the realities around them. But such outward depicting of their observations, thoughts and emotions, implies no spirit of ridicule but rather one of loving understanding. And he who could solve Pearl would not misread the motives of his own Una and Julian.

Inevitably, however, amid their earnest representations, they would give way to childish gossip and gigglings, and to admiration of their own fidelity of imitation. Because their theme was the approach of death, they did not the less find a sort of fun in it. Lightsome, innocent mockery; but to the listener it must sound like mockery nevertheless.

At intervals, Hawthorne, conscious of the strange malady, during the writing of his romance and the playful babble of the two children outdoors, jotted down some of what he heard and felt:

" 'Oh, but, Julian, you don't know how sick she is! She's as sick as I was when I had the fever in Boston!' " And the comment: "That childish ailment—and these last heavy throbbings of my mother's heart!"

Listening to the voices of his children playing outdoors, while innocently mimicking the approach of death to his mother lying in the guest-chamber, Hawthorne continues to jot down impressions surrounding him. He writes: "Una is infinitely adventurous—apt, without warning, to take flight through the street; and is found surrounded by a knot of children who gaze at her with wonder, recognizing that she is not like themselves." And anon, a fresh act of the play: "Una has been fanning flies from her grandmother's face and she now describes it to her brother, who is, meanwhile, riding his new hobby-horse, but attentive. 'It would be too painful for a little boy like Julian to see. Grandma is very sick, indeed.' Julian meditates, and imagines a calamity too grievous even for his sister's maturity of six years: 'How would you feel if little Julian were to faint away, and go to God?' "

Next day another entry: "At my mother's bedside today it was surely the darkest hour I ever lived. And afterward, standing by the open window, the laughter of the children came up into the chamber from outside, and I saw my little Una of the golden locks looking beautiful, and so full of spirit and life that she was very life itself; and between her and my dying mother I seemed to see the whole of human existence at once. Just then, Una's voice came up, very clear and distinct: 'Yes, she is going to die!' "

And later: "There is something about Una that almost frightens me: I know not whether elfish or angelic or supernatural. She steps so boldly into the midst of everything; shrinks from nothing; has a comprehension of everything; at one moment seems to have little delicacy; the next, shows the finest essence of it: now hard—now so tender—now perfectly unreasonable—now again so wise! In certain aspects I cannot believe her my own child, but a spirit, strangely mingled of good and evil, haunting the house where I dwell."

And here at last emerges the enigma of Pearl, in "The Scarlet Letter." The child of Wrath might not have appeared as she does in the story, but for the child of Love and Gladness, who was her sister. But Hawthorne is temperate even in his most radical moods, and by reticence the more powerfully conveys his idea. The

29

conception of an Infant Demon might easily be vulgarized by exaggeration, but Hawthorne, the artist, escapes that error. The story is not of an episode, but of the everlasting struggle in the human heart between Good and Evil; and on a stage so boundless that we may believe (as Hawthorne seems to have done) that it is wiser to pardon than to condemn.

The Union Street House

FROM these sad and vibrant happenings in the Mall Street house, let us consider the unpretentious home of Grandmother Hawthorne, in which Nathaniel himself was born. In Union Street, down by the Salem wharves, stood the original house, built generations before by a Hawthorne ancestor; like many of his predecessors, he owned and commanded ships trading with the Indies, West and East; and Hawthorne wives from windows of their bedrooms could see the vessels as they set forth for the other side of the planet, and, after months, haply returned again.

This little frame house, solidly constructed, still stands, though the Hawthorne ships have vanished, and other people, I believe Polish, occupy the premises. Twenty years ago, when I knocked on the door, the woman who opened it did not invite me in; she had no Hawthorne legends to unfold, and had no doubt been incommoded by previous inquirers. The enlightened plutocrats who are prone to buy such relics and make museums of them had not yet got around to Union Street.

I viewed, from without, the corner windows that look westward, behind which the young Nathaniel Hawthorne wrote the stories afterward collected under the title, "Twice Told Tales." Nearly ninety years had passed since he sat at his desk up yonder, hoping for some intimation from the World outside that what he wrote had been read by somebody besides the proofreader. The intimation came at last; so that he was able to jot down, in his journal, half ironically: "In this dismal chamber fame was won!" A very faint intimation, but after a few years more it was to swell to a chorus, greeting "The Scarlet Letter." The "obscurest man of letters in America," as he had dubbed himself in the preface to "Twice Told Tales," could now be seen and recognized, not in his own country only, but round the world. But by that time he had a wife and children, and fame looked less important than of yore.

As I said, I was not permitted to view that dismal chamber in which fame was won; so I turned away from that ancestral home; but, lest time or fire should destroy it, its portrait has been painted by an artist of genius, who is also my wife, known in the art world as Edith H. Garrigues. The portrait is faithful in every detail, and yet over the whole rests a beauty derived from the sympathy of the painter's soul, which, without belying the commonplace, has a magic to lift it into the ideal.

Visitors—
Book Titles

IN THE renovated Wayside we passed blessed days; the author of "The Scarlet Letter" climbing our hill in the forenoons, to pace his beat along the summit, under the shady boughs, between the sweet-fern and huckleberry bushes; or sitting beside his wife on the broad bench under the white pines looking out over the meadows to Walden woods; or in the summer-house halfway up the slanting path, undergoing, not seldom, respectful interrogations from pious pilgrims, for one of whom he wrote on a card addressed to Mr. Emerson, "This young man seems worthy"—though hardly foreseeing that this humble youth was to become the Dean of American Letters. . . . For another youth, already approved a true poet, he conceived a lifelong friendship, and in a long letter gave him sage advice on the conduct of a campaign to take service under the government. Richard Henry Stoddard showed me that letter a generation afterward, with tears in his dim old eyes: He was born to trouble. Poetry and love were the two highest things to him, and he remained faithful to them to the end. But his poetry, genuine and often moving or exquisite, had no popular appeal, and he had to resort to a federal appointment and to writing literary criticisms to support his family.

A publisher, during Stoddard's last years, issued his collected poems in one volume, and pointing to the book, he said to me, "How many copies do you think were sold in two years? Three!" And then he turned to a certain page and read:

"Life, to me, has been a strange, bewildered dream,
 Wherein I knew not things that be from things that seem!"

So Stoddard and William Dean Howells paused at the Wayside, and passed on; and others, whose names I have forgotten.

When the mood was on him Hawthorne would climb those tower stairs, and shut himself into his study, where two romances were awaiting incarnation, one called provisionally "The Bloody Footstep," the other by various titles—"Septimius," "Doctor Grimshawe" and, finally "The Dolliver Romance." For a time, he meditated combining the two themes into one story, a sort of earthly immortality, the scene being in England, so that he could use material from the journal he had kept while in England. He discarded that plan, and made the seeker for the Elixir a New Englander of British ancestry, living in our Wayside, at the period of the outbreak of the Revolution. But none of these suited him, and for a time he abandoned the romance altogether, and compiled from his journals a book of essays about England—deeming his time for imaginative work was gone by. He was in doubt about the title; and I remember, one evening, that he was pacing to and fro in the little old room that served our family for dining room and "parlor." This room was part of the original dwelling, built perhaps two centuries before. Across the ceiling, which was so low that in 1862 I could

33

lay the palm of my hand on it, extended the ancient oaken beam, such as the builders of those times used for their sturdy house-skeletons. It was characteristic more of the old homes of his ancestors than of their descendants. He loved England, for all its faults, and but for his wish to give his children a chance to grow up Americans, he might never have returned hither from Europe.

He paused in his pacing, and his face cleared, and he said in a deep voice, "Our Old Home!" And we knew he had found what he sought.

He had pondered over titles of former books, but his choice was always good. "Twice Told Tales" was an inspiration, and "The Scarlet Letter." He had at first thought "The House of the Seven Gables" too cumbersome; and "The Blithedale Romance" was more than half written as "Hollingsworth." "The Marble Faun" underwent several vicissitudes. He submitted alternative titles to Smith, Elder & Co., the English publishers, among them "The Transformation of the Faun." They extracted the word "Transformation," and would have nothing else.

Hawthorne didn't care much for the story at first, and had designed it as a short story, or a long-short; but the pressure of his Italian reminiscences made it his longest romance. It was, perhaps, an impossible theme; the mysteries could not be cleared up. But in the end the book found more readers than "The Scarlet Letter," or as many: a work of delicate and profound art, not explicit, but fascinating.

Adventures

YES, we expected to remain at the Wayside forever, but in June of 1853 we were on our way to Liverpool on the little paddle-wheel steamer *Niagara* of the Cunard Line. Though the events of the few following years have appeared in my book "Shapes That Pass," I shall enlarge a little on them here from time to time, especially upon my later friendships, as the pith and color of a personality cannot be confined to a few paragraphs. As for writing an autobiography, I said in that book, and do here repeat, I have no such intention: reminiscences are another matter, for they are the man's experiences, not himself. And they are good tonic for health and spirits.

Two Concord incidents of importance to myself, however, I will rescue from oblivion here; had the issue of them been different, the world would have had to get along without my reminiscences.

Apple trees, set out, I believe, by Bronson Alcott, the former tenant, grew on the hillside at the back of the Wayside, and I used to climb up among the crooked branches to pluck and eat the fruit. But one day my foot slipped, and I was let down between two boughs to just below the ears, and there dangled mute and helpless. Death by hanging is not painful: so much I learned, when my father happened to see me suspended and

35

lifted me out, the apple still in my grip. So Washington had his cherry-tree and I my Baldwin, and we were doubtless greater and wiser men for the experience.

The second adventure was perhaps more sinister. In some past age a local farmer had dug a well beside the highway; it was forty feet deep with six feet of fresh water at the bottom. The farmer died, but the well stayed behind; grass and weeds grew round its margin; some thoughtful person covered with boards the mouth of the shaft. Time passed; rains and sun rotted the boards, moss disguised them; the hole, like the waiting jaws of an unseen monster, bided its time. It was on the south side of the roadway, between it and the rail fence that bounded the meadow beyond. But the hidden well was patient. The American Revolution and the rest of history journeyed by, and the screening planks became more and more invisible, rotten and treacherous. The nameless farmer was to blame in the first place, but the unknown would-be-beneficent busybody who covered the aperture, was the proximate cause of the catastrophe.

A six-year-old urchin, care-free and sharp-eyed, happened to pass that way, descried the moss-covered boards, and, after the manner of such urchins, diverged a little for the pleasure of treading upon them. I don't suppose his weight could have exceeded threescore pounds, but the hour of fate had struck and it was enough. The boards gave way and, a few moments later, splashed into water forty feet below. The urchin was on his way to follow them; but at this juncture instinct took up the tale.

As he went down, he grabbed at the tufts of wiry grass

growing at the edge of the pit. His ancestry had been seafaring men, accustomed to handling rope-ends for weal or woe; his small fingers clutched, and the tough grassroots held. He pulled himself up and, after amusing himself for a while by dropping pebbles into the abyss and hearing them plop, he got to his feet and resumed his journey, care-free as before.

Next day, however, walking beside his father past the spot, he drew him thither and related the incident, not ascribing to it any special importance. "If I had fallen in," he explained, "I could easily have climbed out again by the sticking-out ends of the stones all the way up."

But after the father, bending over, had studied the situation, his face took on a grave expression and he shook his head. He didn't berate his offspring, still less chastise him in the old New England style, such never having been his habit. But he said in tones of unaccustomed seriousness, and therefore the more unforgettable, "No, Julian; if you had fallen down there, you would never have come up again."

That was all, and the subject was never again mentioned between them. But into the soul of Julian entered a deadly chill, never to be entirely banished in the succeeding two and eighty years. Yes, even today, if I allow myself to muse upon the matter, that chill creeps in. Afterwards, in Europe, I stared into the black depths of medieval oubliettes; but they could tell me nothing. My father's "never" planted in me a seed not to be uprooted.

Some thirty years after the incident of the well, into which I all but fell, another rather poignant incident

37

occurred at Etretat on the French coast of the English Channel. Here stand chalk cliffs three hundred feet tall, pierced here and there with pirate caves and stairways of centuries ago. The modern bathing-beach is a gap between two mighty headlands: the western one a huge white dome with a little chapel on its side; the other an extraordinary pinnacle of chalk, upward of a hundred feet sheer, its base covered at high tide but above water at the ebb. The beach here is composed of flint pebbles washed out of the face of the cliffs in the course of countless ages. Beyond the pinnacle westward is another beach, but access to it is rather hazardous—through a hole in the base, just above low-water mark, and with a twist halfway through. The diameter of this hole varies, because after heavy weather loose shingle is piled up within the aperture; but ordinarily there is space enough for an average body to squeeze through, especially in a bathing suit. The length of the crooked passage is about sixty feet.

After my swim one golden afternoon, the sparkle and rhythm of indomitable life being in the sea and air, I was at the peak of my youth and strength; spirit and flesh rejoiced in unison, and all was well; I approached the pinnacle and noticed that the tide was low and the aperture was well above water. I had long meditated trying the passage, and now was my opportunity. I was, however, not in bathing rig, having changed to my suit. I peered into the cavity; I didn't doubt that I could crawl through easily. It was dark within, but the space seemed ample. Before I had gone two yards, however, the light was entirely obscured by my body—the opening at the farther end being hidden by the twist of the passage. Darkness, and no sound except the shifting of the pebbles beneath me. The walls which enclosed me were slimy with seaweed.

At first I was able to go on hands and knees, but I was already flat on my stomach; I felt the scrape of an occasional limpet through the hair on my scalp. I was glad of the cool salt air that I could still breathe; but the pebbles continued to heap up beneath me, and I began to ask myself whether I could get through! My arms were stretched out in front of me, for lack of room to rest on my elbows; I could advance only by a wriggling movement from my knees. I could not go backward, because that would bunch up my coat round my shoulders and at this stage it was impossible to take it off.

All this might be related with ease and laughter in a drawing-room over a cup of afternoon tea, an incident of long ago, when the desperate, long-drawn struggle to escape could be treated half jestingly, to make one's flesh creep. But the thing itself was no jest. It would be difficult to imagine circumstances of death more grim than this. Alone in everlasting dark, hearing the inevitable rising of the tide which in an hour would flood into the narrow crevice where I lay and slowly strangle me out of existence. All around me, on the other side of this immitigable dungeon was the joyous, radiant, lovely, living world, shut against me by a blind door never to be reopened. No one knew of my being there; after some days perhaps some new adventurer, trying the passage, would be halted by an inert mass of clay, slowly disintegrating back into its elements.

I would not surrender; inch by inch I wiggled on, now drenched in sweat. If the end must be death, let it

39

come as far forward as human energy and will could bring it. It was a victory when I found myself at the turn of the tunnel—a far-off glimpse of daylight—but with it the sound of the waves making their first breach through what—if any—must be my gate of deliverance. But the further stages of that journey are obscure in my memory. The space seemed to enlarge somewhat at the last but I arrived none too soon; the final burst was actually under water; I dragged myself feebly out into the untroubled sunlight, and lay in the free air, on the shingle, as on a bed of down. "Weariness can snore upon the flint," says Shakespeare.

Such things make a man acquainted with himself. I was glad of my persistence in physical training. The adventure was curiously like that of the Concord well. I hope that I need no further such reminders of mortal frailty.

Between the last related incident of my life, that of crawling through the hole in the cliff, which so nearly ended my existence, and the episode of the old well, in Concord, about a quarter of a century elapsed. I will say that these gaps and tergiversations are due, first, to the biography written in 1884, "Hawthorne and His Wife" and then to a volume called "Hawthorne and His Circle," which came ten or fifteen years later. It was a collection of odds and ends, into which strayed various personal anecdotes that should have been reserved for the present work; but at that time I had resolved against autobiography. What induced me to change my mind is unimportant; that is what minds are for. One naturally abhors self-repetition; but since none of my readers had yet drawn the breath of life at the time my reminiscences begin (not long after that hot night in Boston in 1846 when I was born, for I began my diaries with pen illustrations of shells, snails and the like when I was seven years old), I will venture to dip occasionally into apt repetition, the better to bridge ungainly jumps. But in fact logical continuity is impracticable in any living story of one's life; and logic and I have never agreed. So, before leaving my first space in Concord, I will recall one thing more, not conducive to my glory, but perhaps of symbolic value; and everything becomes symbolic as our world revolves.

Departure from Concord

ON THE very last evening before our family entrained for Boston on our way to England (a warm evening in June it was, with the sun, as is its habit at that season, setting late), I, being congenitally shy of company, privately resolved to have a bath. A little company of friendly ladies and gentlemen had assembled to bid us farewell. I supposed them to be in the living-room, which was too near my bedroom to suit my modesty, so I carried my tin tub around into the outhouse, and had a good secluded splash there. But I had forgotten my towel; and returning by the back way, who of all persons should I encounter but Ann, the cook!

She was a maiden of mature years and strict views. I was totally unclothed and quite as strict in my views and habits, at six years of age as she was at sixty. We both uttered exclamations of horror, and I turned about and, without reflecting, sought to escape around the front of the house. In my agitation I had forgotten the ladies and gentlemen! The rays of the declining sun dazzled my eyes. Suddenly I was in the midst of muslin frocks, summer bonnets, black coats and top hats. I was aware of a stir, sounds of surprise, perhaps of cachinnation: but it would be vain to retreat, and ignoble to run. My belief is that I stalked forward stiff-legged, like those walking-stick insects which I long afterward became acquainted with in the West Indies—in fact a Cupid unmitigated. In my friend Herman Melville's "Typee" or "Omoo" the episode would have passed unnoticed; but I realized thus early the pains of the White Man's Burden.

The next morning was another day, and before the sun set again we were far out upon the Atlantic, and the Burden dropped overboard. Left behind, too, were those midsummer temperatures of 112 degrees. Today science and civilization abate our hardships; but that was not the case in New England eighty-two years ago. Nor could we soothe ourselves with thinking of a Land whose rocks and rivers glittered with Virgin Gold. There were no Forty-niners then, nor covered wagons. We were busy recovering from the American Revolution, and the young Ralph Waldo Emerson had hardly yet composed his Hymn to the Embattled Farmers. I was born at the time when General Zach Taylor was leading his little army against Mexico; was fourteen when Sumter surrendered, and a Harvard undergraduate when Lincoln died. Queen Victoria of England had fifty years yet to reign; the great World War was not yet imagined; persons and events which are household words today

were unseen and unheard then: the twentieth century
was a remote Phantom of the Dawn. And when I look
back over the sands of Time which my feet have trod,
I seem incredible even to myself.

And I dare say preceding Rip Van Winkles have had
like doubts. Only today is; yesterday and tomorrow are
insubstantial visions; Shakespeare spoke of human history when he said, "full of sound and fury, signifying
nothing!" Einstein says today will come back to us,
after making the circuit of the light year. And perhaps
it won't matter much if it doesn't.

My Uncle Horace Mann
—Elizabeth Peabody

YOU will observe that the ensuing chapters are devoted mainly to the education of the protagonist, and
it may sadden you to learn that his education must still
be put off to his fourteenth year. Most boys of that age,
nowadays, are all-but or quite men grown; have selected
their trade or profession, and may even be drawing
wages. How happens it, then, that a New England youth
of fortunate environment should be so long delayed in
making a start?

My uncle Horace Mann advocated universal education for both sexes. He worked for it all his life, and in
1858 was president of Antioch College, which started
the new fashion. He was very strenuous, and, to those
who disagreed with his principles, a bit intolerant and

43

faddish; he told my father, whom he found smoking a cigar, that he could no longer feel the respect for his moral character which he had till then entertained; and after examining the skull conformation of his youngest son, told the infant's mother that he was not worth bringing up. She (my mother's sister), though idolizing her husband, failed to destroy the infant, who, in the sequel, became a distinguished entomologist and a natural-history magnate in Washington. As for my father, he arched an eyebrow and finished his cigar; though I must admit that a box of them, of the best Havana leaf, presented to him by Franklin Pierce, lasted him four or five years—and friends of ours, including Pierce himself, consumed several of these. But Horace Mann's educational idea caught on, as everybody knows.

There is a school with his name on the front of it in many cities of America. I remember him well; a tall, lean man, with stiff, dry, pale hair, a wide mouth and shiny spectacles. He and I didn't approve of each other, but I knew he was a good man, even after surprising him one morning in the act of shaving. He died while we were abroad; of his three sons, Horace, the eldest, became an ardent worshiper of the great Agassiz; George, the second, graduated in my class at Harvard, and spent the rest of his life as principal of a girls' school; Benjamin Pickman, the youngest, was a fellow pupil of mine in Frank Sanborn's famous boy-and-girl school in Concord. We called him Picky; a quaint, odd, mischievous, lovable little humorist he was, very like a Cruikshank caricature, a Rumpelstiltzkin of the Brothers-Grimm vintage.

"But O, but O," as Shakespeare sings, "The hobby-horse is forgot!" I was speaking of education. In the

Horace Mann sense I was uneducated at fourteen, in spite of my father and my mother, my Aunt Elizabeth Peabody, a devoted English governess, and later an American one. The English little Miss Brown was an amiable little nobody who knew nothing—not even as much as my sisters Una and Rose and myself did; she dropped off betimes; she pronounced "parallelogram" with the accent on the *o*, and would affirm that the square of the hypotenuse was equal to the square of the two limbs. Under the guidance of Ada Sheppard, the American governess, who was a graduate of Antioch and who knew everything but did not possess the teaching gift, we learned by heart Macaulay's "Lays of Ancient Rome." We were living in Rome at the time; and it was while sitting romantically with her in the Palace of the Caesars that Una caught the germs of the Roman fever, which all but ended her life and never entirely left her.

It was my custom to arise at dawn and walk along the high banks of the turbulent yellow Tiber, which the brave Horatius once swam, and where the lean and hungry Cassius once bore on his shoulders the tired Caesar—if that anecdote of his to Brutus is true. Two thousand years ago!—and the dome rounded by the hand of Michael Angelo fifteen hundred years later lifted itself above the shadows of the sleeping city into the clear Roman sky.

Now as to Aunt Elizabeth Peabody: She was short and wide without being exactly fat and was heedless of her personal attire; she had soft brown hair floating away from her capacious head, loving gray eyes behind spectacles, and a tender mouth. She was empty of purse but rich beyond measure in beneficence to all needy persons, who, accordingly, always clustered about her with palms outstretched, physically or metaphorically. She was deceived a thousand times but never lost faith. She was probably the most learned person in the world —certainly the most learned woman, in an era of feminine pundits. It was she who, as you may know, introduced kindergartens from Germany and superintended a string of them in Boston. Greek, Latin, Sanskrit and Hebrew were household tongues with Aunt Lizzie. And not content with knowing things, she wanted everybody else to know them, and had invented ingenious ways of instructing them.

To proceed with my remarkable Aunt Elizabeth Peabody. She taught me ancient history, dates and all, by colored diagrams, without my knowing that I was being taught. Here was old Plato's Day in yellow and purple: this scarlet square is the birthday of Julius Caesar, 102 B.C. You will recall that it was she who helped to bring me into the world; and after I had grown up and married, she periodically wrote me long letters on thin paper, crossed and sometimes recrossed (it was the fashion of the day) counseling me on matters. I seldom read and seldomer answered this wisdom, but she was never discouraged.

When she was seventy years old, but with a soul as young as in her girlhood, some rich person gave her $500, with the proviso that she was to spend it solely on herself. She went to Europe on a three months' visit, all alone, and with no more luggage than would go into a portable bag. She had a glorious time, and came back radiant. I wish I could tell of this marvelous pilgrimage. Not since the Saints of Christendom journeyed over the earth has there been anything like it. Her progress was a continual miracle: no mishap from start to finish; she came back transfigured, and for ten years afterward would recount her adventures to loving listeners. The last time I saw her was on the threshold of a little hut in Concord; she stood in her wrapper, her soft gray hair floating down her back, her face seraphic with holy purpose. As I turned at the gate, she threw up her right arm and called out, "I am the champion of the Indians!" She said it half laughingly, for she was never deficient in the sense of humor; but she meant it! She had already, during and after the Civil War, valiantly vindicated the rights of the Negroes. But the ways of God are unsearchable. She was never married, but she was one of the Mothers of mankind.

I count my Aunt Lizzie, then, as eminent among my pre-Sanborn teachers. But my aesthetic culture began with my mother in the nursery. She, too, was learned; a prodigious reader and a deep and original thinker, but not a thesaurus of all knowledge like her sister, Aunt Lizzie. She had a great gift in the fine arts, and was a pupil of Washington Allston and of others eminent in sculpture and painting in her day. Emerson, his face a wise light, used to look in and converse with her for a few minutes, remarking that the Muses were in the woods today; and other contemporaries of the period, the Channings, and other monarchs of the New England nobility, used to call. They were drawn to her as to an angel visiting earth, who brought out in them good which they had not known they possessed, yet who was always in the posture of receiving rather than dispensing; but she was keen and fearless and full of delicate humor, and often discomfited their human logic with Divine reasons which opened heavenly vistas.

Learning at Home
—Writing

BUT then, one day, as related in a letter from her sister Elizabeth to me, she was induced, reluctantly, to receive Nathaniel Hawthorne, some of whose writings she had read; a man who was very shy, but who, in her presence, let fall jewels of beauty and insight. Her soul recognized its mate and master, and she instinctively drew back, as from the unexpected incarnation of dreams reserved for Paradise. And he saw in her a flower too exquisite for mortal gathering. True love is embarrassed in the presence of love and feels a mutual unworthiness, as if acceptance must be descent to walk rough-shod in the inmost shrines of holiness. But by and by the celestial music harmonizes with the human, and life, in its simplicity, becomes a continuous miracle. From the time they met, her health improved, and after their marriage and as long as he lived, the invalid was seldom ill. All this and more transpired afterward in the widow's conversations with her children.

She taught me to believe in good and to see beauty. We had a folio volume of engravings of designs of classic subjects by Flaxman, which the Peabodys had just received the night Nathaniel Hawthorne paid his first visit to their household. These I studied inexhaustibly,

48

and she told the immortal stories which they figured
and encouraged my childish copyings of the designs.
But this art training also begot in me precise acquaintance with the proportions and details of the perfect
human figure, which was later to be substantiated by
the sculpture galleries of Rome, Paris and London; so
that before I reached my teens, I knew what the body
and carriage of a man ought to be. And I have thought
since then that life-size casts of those classic statues
should stand in all our public schools. They would do
more good than does our present system of competitive
athletics, which develops monstrosities and saps vitality.

As for reading, writing and arithmetic, they seemed
to come by nature, but certainly not prematurely; I
think there were new methods—Germanic probably—
which seemed to make such things grow spontaneously,
and which Aunt Lizzie lovingly cultivated in me. But
in my twelfth year, being then in England, my father
tightened his belt and set out to teach me Latin. Long
before that, however, he had made all us children familiar with English literature.

Not by modern methods of intensive study, however
—nothing like that. In fact, there was, in our family,
no such thing as study. There is a natural process known
as endosmosis: two substances not mutually antagonistic
are placed side by side, and flow into each other through
an intervening medium; that is the idea, never mind
the details. But the appropriation is involuntary and
pleasurable: like the business man in Molière's comedy
—amazed to find that he had been talking prose all his
life though he had never learned it; and I remember

my own surprise when I first was in Paris at hearing small children chattering French.

So when my father, of an evening, in his easy-chair beside the lamp, would take up a book and begin reading aloud to his wife and children the poetry and prose that live forever—Milton and Shakespeare, Spenser and Scott, Macaulay and De Quincey, Wordsworth and Tennyson, the legends of Old Pelops' Line and the Tale of Troy divine—to have thought of this as study, in the Horace Mann sense, would have been outrage. The type of true education is the Tree, growing from within outward, endogenously. The posters and road signs plastered on from without may be useful in their way, but never become part of the tree; they may kill it. But such doctrine was more popular in ancient Greece than here and now.

My father was the best reader I ever listened to: Charles Dickens was as powerful but with less refinement; the American romancer wielded the scimitar of Saladin rather than the two-handed broadsword of Richard Cœur de Lion. The spirit of what they were reading passed into the faces of both, a thing indescribable and incredible, like the soul itself, which we may deny, but it Is! Of the two, Hawthorne was the stronger nature, though immeasurably less resonant and explicit —deeper but less vivid. Have our professors of today read and digested—lived through and into—the whole series of the Waverley Novels, for instance, or "The Lay of the Last Minstrel" and its companions? But did they know them in childhood or early youth? For after that enchanted period the gates are closed, never to be reopened. "What does it prove?" asked the Oxford scholar, after glancing over "Paradise Lost." And for this kind of ignorance there is no remedy in earth or heaven. The outer Darkness is crowded with such.

But Latin was another story. My father enjoyed the language and had specialized in it at Bowdoin; and it may have helped purify his style afterward. He now produced a small, worn volume of one of the minor Latin authors, and we set to work.

Did we have grammar? We must have had, but I have no recollection of such a thing until long afterward, in Sanborn's school. Neither did I, then or ever, possess or look into a grammar of the English tongue. I cannot account for this, but I never missed it. Of course, I never had any intention of becoming an author; that was, apparently, a pure accident that happened long afterward, and I had been one for some years before I was conscious of it. In fact, at first, I didn't take myself seriously in literature, and chance and inclination have been my guides through life. I did take engineering seriously, labored at it in the Harvard Lawrence School after my class had graduated and gone home, in 1867; went to the Realschule in Dresden, Saxony, to complete my preparation, returned to New York and was an employee of General George B. McClellan for a year. When he was retired for political reasons, I went with him; and it was while awaiting a new appointment that I happened, just for fun, to write a short story.

When *Harper's* sent me $50 for it and asked for more, I was astonished but complied, finding myself full of such yarns; the emoluments seemed good, and between the Harper periodicals and *Appleton's Journal,* and no other engineering appointment, I have kept on till the present day. But it all seemed an accident, and "fun"— though, of course, once in a while I would hit upon a theme that really interested me, and the game became serious. I don't defend such a course, nor recommend it to the deadly-serious young persons who nowadays choose writing for a profession.

It may have been "chance" or "fun" that made me an author, but I have burned the midnight oil; I once had to write an entire novelette of 26,000 words in twenty-six consecutive hours, and it came out as good as the average of my stuff; and I once wrote a 60,000 word novel, "Fortune's Fool," in competition for a $10,000 prize, finishing it in twenty-one days, and got the prize—at a time, too, when I needed the money. And what with fiction, biography, history, journalism, and poetry, I suppose that what I have put on paper during the last sixty-odd years might fill at least one hundred bound volumes. Some of the poetry, of which there is quite a good deal, seemed to me to be pretty good, but very little of it is in print.

So the moral of my career seems to be that doing a thing for fun does not guarantee an easy job. On the other hand I found it very enjoyable; and it has brought me the acquaintance and often the friendship of scores of the finest men and women in the world; whereas, as an engineer I might have fallen into politics and become President of the United States; and such people are bound, I presume, to take themselves seriously, and to do without friends.

Meanwhile, what about my Latin? If I had no grammar, I did have a dictionary, and was told to look up the words. But many Latin words bear an outward resemblance to English ones; and looking up words in Andrews and Stoddart's huge English-Latin Lexicon is hard work. So when the Latin author said that the messengers, traveling by relays, finished their journey "continuo cursu," and I considered the difficulties of the undertaking, I needed no dictionary to interpret the passage, and informed my father that the riders completed their journey with "continual cursing." Upon which he burst into shouts and roars of Homeric laughter, throwing himself back in his chair and kicking up his feet. I joined in the explosion without understanding the joke—as many others have done before and since; a laugh being a laugh, sense or not. A correct translation would have been much less worth while. But I think ordinary conscientious pedagogues would have dissented from this view.

My uncle Horace Mann, for example, after penalizing me for my negligence, would have gone on to say that the passage freely construed meant that the messengers would have changed horses at every station, and would thus have been able to do the whole distance at a gallop. "Continuo cursu"—at top speed all the way. Of course they might have used bad language on the side, but my uncle would not have admitted it. And I would have forgotten the whole matter next day, whereas my father's reaction has caused me to remember it after two and eighty years. It may not have been worth remembering; but that is not the point.

PART TWO

Concord and Its Famous
Personalities

Amos Bronson Alcott

THE Alcotts and the Emersons were our neighbors; but the Alcotts lived next door, while the Emersons were half a mile away. I will tell first about the Alcotts: live people can't be fenced into chapters, however; in the web of events they appear and vanish at hazard.

Mr. Alcott dressed—rather, Mrs. Alcott dressed him —all in white, or in black, according to the season. She made, or at least remade, his garments; such being the way in old New England; trousers were turned inside out and coats refurbished. In April, Mr. Alcott would amble off into the woods back of his house, and come back with a bundle of fagots, which he would presently transform into a fence or a summer-house, avoiding straight lines, and showing artistic judgment in curves and bends. His tools were a hatchet, a saw, a hammer, and a keg of nails. Mr. Wetherbee, the village carpenter, said that Mr. Alcott consumed more nails in making a fence than any other man would require to construct a two-story house, shingles included. Alcott's arbors and fences came costless from his brain, and Mrs. Alcott, a wise housekeeper, kept him supplied with nails, no matter what else must be economized.

Amos Bronson Alcott wrote a good deal, and at the end of his ninety years he composed a little volume of sonnets on his friends. He had been a contributor to the *Dial* of long before; and even the *Atlantic* found space for some of his "Orphic Sayings." But the man couldn't write, for all Emerson's efforts to show him how: he couldn't put the grace and originality of his fences into prose. He turned out a pretentious rodomontade of platitudes; Nature, which did half the fences for him, could not help him otherwise; though, curiously, those sonnets, which were strictly conventional in form, showed good observation of character, and were even passable as literature.

What he did in the room set apart for his study was never known; he spent hours daily there, and was not to be interrupted. He was well supplied with pens and ink and paper, and books, but none of the last was of his making.

You remember Charles Lamb's story about Coleridge, who, meeting him on the street, began to talk, holding on to him by the upper button of his coat, and closing his eyes, as was his habit. Lamb, by and by, having urgent affairs elsewhere, sliced the button off his coat and left it in his friend's finger and thumb, and stole away unnoticed. Returning after some hours, he found Coleridge still confiding to the button the mysteries of philosophy unaware of what had happened on the material plane. Alcott's urge to impart wisdom might have been similarly appeased, and adequate buttons might have been provided; but we were short of Charles Lambs at that place. Besides, there really were groups of persons, mostly ladies, who would sit and listen to Alcott, world without end.

Mr. Alcott, as many of us know, never ate anything but bread and milk and apples and raw vegetables. I will quote a poem, apropos of that. It was composed by a friend who lived next door, who was seldom stirred to verse save on high occasions, and it happened at a time when the Edward Lear nonsense rhymes had captured us and we were all busy trying to imitate them. The children next door to the Alcotts caught the contagion and applied to the gentleman in question for a contribution. Paper and pencil were supplied on the spot, and he wrote:

> There lived a Sage at Apple-Slump
> Whose dinner never made him plump;
> Give him carrots, potatoes, squash, turnips and peas,
> And a handful of crackers without any cheese,
> And a cup of cold water to wash down all these,
> And he'd prate of the spirit as long as you please,
> This airy sage of Apple-Slump.

I have often thought that if those small blinking eyes of Alcott's had been replaced by a pair like those of Goethe for instance, Amos Bronson Alcott would have been one of the most tremendous figures in our history. He would have conquered these United States and established a new religion. But he had to make his way without the imperial dominating glance. Even so, he stands out as a remarkable and memorable personage, who "obeyed at eve, the voice obeyed at prime," and really gained in moral and intellectual stature as he advanced in age.

His persistent conviction that human nature was capable of housing the godhead amused the many, astonished some, and exasperated a few. Among the last group, on one occasion at least, was Henry James the elder, a powerful character, a wit, humorist, and a profound student and expositor of the fundamental secrets of religion.

"Did you ever say," he broke out at Alcott, when the latter had been particularly orphic on his favorite theme, "Did you ever say, 'I am the Resurrection and the Life'?"

Alcott blinked but replied bravely and mildly, "Yes, Mr. James, I have said that."

James looked at him for a moment with the stern joy of a warrior who finds a foe to stand up to the battle-axe, and rejoined, "Did anyone ever believe on you?"

But Alcott believed on himself nevertheless.

Ages before the small boy, who was myself, came into contact with him, Alcott had kept school. It was designed to solve the problem of the training of youth; and it would have succeeded but for a single oversight: the pupils were not all little Alcotts. And those acquainted with the family history know that the distinctive feature of the school was that when any pupil did wrong chastisement followed; but it was upon the teacher, not upon the delinquent, that it was inflicted. Alcott believed that the heart of the child would be touched and reformed by the spectacle of his schoolmaster suffering for another's misdeeds, even as Christ had suffered for the world's sin, and the Alcottism would thus become a supplement to Christianity.

The pupils multiplied their iniquities for the fun of seeing the master thrash himself, and it ceased after a while without having regenerated a single scholar.

Alcott had been born a thousand years too soon. How was such a man to make his way in the world? No doubt he underwent severe privations, but he was more constant than Galileo, and would have died rather than recant.

He married a woman of beauty and charm and of great practical good sense, for whom and for his gifted and agreeable daughters I was much indebted to him. The Alcott house, with its spacious low-ceilinged living-room, wide fireplace, piano and kitchen, was just the place for what we called "parties," and my sisters and I were often invited; or we would drop in and the party would begin. There were dances—polka, schottische, lancers, waltz—with Louisa or Abbie at the piano; or we would sit at the big round table and play long-whist (the modern varieties were not then invented), euchre, old-maid, and other games.

Abbie and I were partners, as a rule, and would cheat industriously. Then Mrs. Alcott would come in from the kitchen, and the cards gave way to root-beer (home-made), cakes, and pies of the old, deep-dish sort; and finally, if it was fall or winter we would get about the fireplace, and Louisa would tell stories. She was incomparable at that—wit and humor, drama, and especially that tale of murder and a ghost, when the candles would be suddenly blown out, and a death-scream yelled out to stop your heartbeat. This was before the conception or writing of "Little Women,"— a fortunate book for later ages! But as for Mr. Alcott, one thing is certain: there was nobody else like him in the world.

Louisa and Abbie Alcott

WHEN I first saw Louisa Alcott, she was a black-haired, red-cheeked, long-legged hobbledehoy though not looking her twenty-eight years or seeming near that age. But there was power in her jaw, control in her black eyes, good nature in her generous mouth, and jollity in her laugh; in short, she was a leader. Honesty, good will and common sense were the breath of her nostrils; penetration, too; and humor surpassing the ordinary humor of women—an attitude of comedy in her daily conversation, but poised and inwardly sparkling.

All these good qualities finally assembled themselves into the gift of writing stories about girls and boys. Her greatest success, "Little Women," was published in the late sixties, and recently it was filmed for audiences who had read the book in their childhood. Fifty years of popularity lasting over to our revolutionary and sophisticated twentieth century! A book written just after the Civil War, and keeping good all through the World War! Nothing short of genius could have achieved such results.

Louisa's success was immediate, and was entirely a surprise to her. Hawthorne called himself in one of his early prefaces, "the obscurest man of letters in America."

Alcott could have contended with him for that distinction, but he was the father of the most popular woman author America has produced: "The Scarlet Letter" won fame but never had a tithe of the readers of "Little Women." The sale of the book rescued the family from real poverty, and Louisa, who had a romantic imagination and longed to write tales of wild passion and adventure, had the judgment and self-control to continue the simple and homely vein in which she had begun. Volume followed volume, and the family never afterward lacked the comforts of life.

In the midst of her home activities came the Civil War, and Louisa went to the front as a nurse. Her journal of that experience, "Hospital Sketches," was later published. But after she was brought home from the war, and lay for a long time between life and death, with the memory of her terrible days haunting her, a hollow-eyed and almost fleshless wreck of the Louisa we had known and loved—after her slow convalescence, climbing painfully out of the grave to life, she was not the same girl who had left us a year before. During the twenty years of her literary activity that followed, she remained as it were behind a veil; occasionally it would slip aside for a while, and a flash of humor or a shaft of wit would come out of the shadow. Her experiences influenced her writing, manifestly mellowed and deepened it; she could not have touched a million hearts except from the depth of her own. But the price she paid was great.

Between Louisa's sister Abbie and myself there was formed a private alliance. I should perhaps confess that there had been a tacit understanding in the two families

that Abbie (May) and I were to be romantically attached, though in fact it was one of the inter-family
jokes, fostered by Louisa. At all events, I assumed airs
of proprietorship over Abbie.

She said she would marry any man who would take
her to Europe to study art. Nothing, at the time, seemed
less probable; but it is pleasant to record that long after
these Concord days, the man actually appeared and fulfilled her dream. For the moment we had our little
romantic episodes. Thoreau had told me one day when
we were standing on the rock at North Branch, where
a smaller stream joins Concord River—a picturesque
spot, where a tall, precipitous bank overhung the still,
black surface of the water, crowned with dark pines,
and with scarlet cardinal flowers on the opposite bank,
sheaves of which my father used to gather for his bride,
in their Old Manse honeymoon in the 1840's: and where
white water-lilies with golden hearts lay on their broad
green pads on the smooth sable mirror—Thoreau, I say,
had told me that the lilies closed their petals at sunset,
but in the morning, as the first rays of the sun touched
them, they stirred and awoke, and, from green buds,
became glorious blooms. "Worth seeing!" said Thoreau,
turning upon me his "terrible blue eyes," as Emerson
called them. All the strange man said was gospel to me,
and I silently resolved to get up early some morning,
and witness that exquisite drama. And the thought of
Abbie naturally came with this resolve.

The sun got up early in New England Julys. North
Branch was a long mile from the Wayside. Abbie was
not spontaneously an early riser. But I recalled an adventure with Ada Sheppard (our governess) at Rome
of tying a string to her ankle by which to arouse her, the

other end hanging out of the window. I proposed it to Abbie and she consented to the Roman experiment. In the transparent dusk before dawn I twitched the magic cord, and the princess responded. She was not only endlessly good-natured, but her artistic and romantic sympathies were aroused: she came smiling down in a pretty white muslin frock, and we were on our way while the rest of the world slept. And you shall soon hear all about our adventure.

As I was saying, I arranged with Abbie to see Thoreau's mystic lilies, and called her at dawn one morning. Abbie, smiling, and like a white violet in her muslin frock, came down for our adventure—the dew was on the grass; but Abbie picked up her skirts, and with the pussycat-like dexterity of women, escaped the stains of travel.

We arrived, full of poetry and romance. The little punt was lying drawn up among the cardinals; the sun had risen in a clear sky, but was not yet high enough to touch the black river and its lovely burden. Abbie stepped into the punt; she was not a fairylike person, nor acrobatic, and the punt responded sensibly to her presence; and when I had climbed into the bow I felt need of circumspection. I pushed out cautiously, intimidated by the spotless muslin frock. Abbie was joyous, and impatient for the drama to begin. The current of the stream was barely perceptible here, and the lily-pads themselves served as moorings: there were scores of them around us. Now let Phoebus Apollo perform his miracle!

What if Thoreau had romanced—not with his customary punctilious accuracy! The punt rocked as the misgiving crossed my mind—so teetery were we. The river, impenetrable to the eye, might have been as unfathomable as the lake where the castle of Chillon stands—a thousand fathoms, according to the poet. I had once swum in front of Chillon, but I had not had Abbie to carry. I hastened to reflect that Thoreau could not have been in a jesting mood; never in his life did he condescend to such a thing. We pushed on, and the sun kept on rising.

At last, a slender shaft of light touched a lily-bud. Did it stir? The trouble, as I now saw it, was going to be that the sheltered bend where the lilies grew could not at once be irradiated, as they would be on the open reaches of the river, where Thoreau had been used to observing them. There could be no sudden unveiling and resurrection of the entire plantation here.

However, that first bud was by this time really opening, and the others must follow, as the shining sword of the god gave them the divine accolade. I paddled the punt to a convenient point, and Abbie reached out. She caught the stem, and hauled in with a cry of triumph, unsuspicious of ill. The stem resisted her pull (we all know their tenacity), and the punt leaned slowly and irrecoverably toward disaster; as we went over, it occurred to me that it would be difficult swimming with those long, tough stems coiling round my legs. Abbie was no naiad, but she behaved well. One scream came from her, ending in a gurgle, and then we both struck bottom—not a thousand fathoms, but a good three feet. The punt had floated lightly off, but we no longer needed it. We waded ashore on our own, the hard-won lily still in Abbie's hand.

But the real calamity was not the upset. Of the depth

66

through which we waded, two and a half feet were slimy black mud, which stained like ink. My breeches didn't matter; but Abbie's muslin whiteness could never be redeemed. And even that was not the worst; for Concord folk were early risers, and we must run the gantlet of a dozen or more front yards and windows on our homeward journey. Our secret adventure would become open history.

But the stainless fact emerges that Abbie never, then or later, complained. Good nature of that degree is unique in my experience. She laughed with a heartiness that her guardian angels must have smiled to hear. It was no hollow cachinnation, but honest mirth. Admirable girl! my heart went out to her. And in addition to her hopeless, bedraggled petticoats, she insisted on bearing all the blame. As for the water-lily, she took it home and preserved it for days in a bowl,—not, certainly as a *memento mori;* rather might it symbolize a charity in the *ewig Weibliche* that can never die.

A Bathing Party
at Walden Pond

THE Alcott house, Apple-Slump, stood upward of a hundred yards west of the Wayside, not flush with the roadway, but withdrawn some twenty paces, and overshadowed by two superb old trees on either side the doorway. A grassplot intervened, and then the rustic fence, Mr. Alcott's handiwork and masterpiece. Behind the house rose a wooded hillside, to match our own on the east; and a wood-path wound away between them.

Our hill plunged steeply down to the roadway—the old Concord-Boston turnpike, the Paul Revere road, a twenty-mile stretch, with Lexington on the way. For the accommodation of the two households, a footpath had been made along the base of the acclivity, passing a couple of small hollows, once cellar-holes of huts which Time had devoured before our era: in which my father had planted sunflowers, that throve exceedingly and smiled upon the passer-by.

And here I take up my tale. Going on my schoolward way one morning I met Abigail May Alcott, pleasant-faced, with yellow-brown curls down her shoulders. She wanted to be called "May," but the jinx which controls such matters perversely insisted on Abigail, though compromising on "Abbie." She was humorously disposed, though not, like Louisa, an original humorist; she had a wide mouth and small but friendly gray eyes. I knew her but slightly at the time of our meeting on the road: she was seven or eight years older than I, but I was physically well-grown, and the young lady took me at eye-value. As our dialogue proceeded she presently enquired, "Do you like ladies and gentlemen bathing together?"

For a moment I stared dumb-stricken, visions of orgiastic revels rioting through my brain. I was fresh from England, where naked improprieties were unthinkable. But Abbie's untroubled gaze met mine without a quiver, and reason began to resume her seat in my distracted globe: it must be all right somehow. Abbie was manifestly in favor of the adventure, and she went on to say, "The Emersons will be along, and I'm going to get your sisters to join us." I was late for school, and jog-trotted westward, rearranging my ideas.

That was seventy-odd years ago; the other day I walked on the California beach where I am passing the summer. The bathing-costumes of the young ladies reminded me of the epigram on the baby who died too soon: "If I so soon was to be done for, I wonder what I was begun for!" But the young gentlemen who attended them were similarly attired, and nobody seemed to mind. And yet I thought that if we of 1860 could have been suddenly brought over to the 1930's there would be something doing. Time tempers the winds of fashion to the shorn lamb.

However, our little party assembled on the shore of Walden Pond on the Saturday after my interview with Abbie. Near by was the deserted hut that Thoreau had built, and from which he had been ousted by the Concord authorities for nonpayment of taxes, A lovely cup of coolness the little lake was, a mile in diameter, a hundred feet deep, surrounded by the dark pine forest. There was a virginal mystery about this translucent lake; it had no inlet or outlet; but every seven years the water rose quietly, covering the narrow shore of white sand and, after some days, again subsiding: a deep, silent, tranquil breath. Winds seldom reached its surface, protected by the high summits of the primeval pines. A maiden lake, slumbering under an enchanted spell.

But we were a holiday party, come for a good time. We made a tent for the young ladies by wrapping cotton sheets round the trunks of four pines which stood con-

veniently at the corners of a square, put in the bundles
of bathing-suits, and then went behind a thick clump
of bushes to put on our jerseys and pantaloons. Then
I strolled off by myself, and gave a few moments' rein to
imagination.

I had been brought up on Classic Fable, and the
vision came spontaneously. Thoreau's hut was a little
Greek temple, dedicated to Aphrodite, on an inlet of
the Aegean Sea. From the wood emerged a troupe of
fauns and bacchantes, the sunlight glowing on the naked
beauty of their bodies as they came dancing and singing
forth from the shadow of the trees. Into the clear water
they plunged with laughter and shouting, diving and
disporting dolphinlike, ivory-white. And yonder drew
near the Goddess herself, her immortal form poised in
the hollow shell, fanned forward by the wings of doves.

"All right, fellows!" sang out Ned Bartlett. "The
ladies are ready!" Four thousand years rolled up like a
scroll, and we are here because, as the poet sang, we are
here!

Ned Bartlett's shout that the ladies were ready brought
me back from imagination to fact: six mid-Victorian
divinities swathed from throat to ankle, inclusive, in
honest dark-blue flannel! Their hair, except Louisa
Alcott's, was coiled into caps; she, with the audacity of
genius, let the masses of her raven locks tumble to her
hips. Edith Emerson, most fastidious, had covered her
feet with slippers; but the others had left theirs—as dear
old Mrs. Hoyden would have said—"puffickly stark-bare-
naked!" A subtle recklessness is prone to creep into us,
in harmony with the perilous freedom of natural surroundings.

70

"Don't you think it's much nicer with ladies and gentlemen together?" said Abbie. We had pushed out from the shore in an old punt.

At that moment the punt careened violently to starboard: Louisa, swimming at large, had grabbed the gunwale to clamber in. The little craft had been built to hold one, or two at a pinch; it capsized amid shouts, screams and splashings; and I, diving deep beneath the glassy, cool, translucent water, escaped replying to Abbie's inquiry. But I afterward learned that Louisa Alcott, in her struggle to get aboard, had split one leg of her flannel pantaloons from hip to knee, revealing a flash of living white amid the blue! One could but be thankful it hadn't happened to Edith Emerson. Louisa simply laughed in the most impenitent way: Ellen Emerson, always self-controlled, drew her within the protection of the tent for repairs.

Reviewing this episode of bathing in Walden Pond, from a distance, I am inclined to think that 1860 gave us as much fun as the 1930's could. Imagination is all right, but some things aren't done, even when we seem to be doing them. If, in place of our young ladies, we had had the company of Miss California, Miss New York, Miss America, and even of Miss Universe, there would have been no real gain, and there might have been an aftermath. Blue flannel may not be beautiful in itself; but neither is reality equal to imagination. What Paradise may be, we can find out only by waiting for it.

There will be plenty to tell of our young ladies as we go on; I must take events as they occur to me.

There was Sam Hoar, for example, scion of a distinguished line. He was a grandson of the venerable

71

Samuel Hoar, who dated from the Revolution, and who wore the garments of 1789, tastefully modified by later fashions; the very tall black beaver, high-coiled black stock, close-waisted black coat, and urbane manners. He had been eminent in the law for sixty years. He was born in 1770 and died in 1862. To meet his bland and courteous presence smiling down the village street was like taking a bath in the pure waters of ancient history.

Sam was also the nephew of the admirable and honored Senator George Frisbie Hoar, immovable in Congress and always on the right side. Finally, he was the son of Judge Ebenezer Rockwood Hoar, whose name was like the granite-bound region of his birth, upright and immitigable as the Law and the Prophets and possessor of the shiningest and most penetrating pair of spectacles in New England. He bore himself in public with an appalling politeness; but fancy the culprit facing him on the Bench! Even the jurors must have sat with their souls in their boots. But we shall see him from another angle before I end this tale.

Sam Hoar

SO WE arrive at Sam Hoar himself, the Sam of our school, and perhaps the best liked of us all. Even Sanborn found him irresistible, and condoned his shortcomings, being aware of his hardships. Yet in the eyes of his father Sam was a lamentable outlaw; he loved him of course, but all the more felt bound to lambaste him in old Biblical fashion. Sam took his punishment grimly but went on smoking just the same, and would even chew into the bargain. These were about the sum of his iniquities; he had no taste for drink, and he was free from vicious practices; but tobacco he would have, in spite of the Law, the Prophets, the Constitution of the United States, and Judge Ebenezer Rockwood Hoar, spectacles, birch, and all. I'm not sure that he really cared so much for the weed as he did for personal liberty. Very likely Patrick Henry and he might have got on together like a house afire.

We all knew the situation; Sanborn knew it, and no doubt agreed with the Judge as to the evil of tobacco, but would not interfere: Sam never complained. Sam was a boys' boy, and rather precocious in manhood. With the village people he was popular, he was democratic and witty, and in the tiny shop of Jonas Hastings, the bootmaker, three or four of the free spirits of the school would often meet and cultivate the seeds of freedom. Jonas made first-rate boots: Mr. Emerson was one of his customers, and when Emerson gave a lecture at the Town Hall, Jonas would always be present and applausive.

When war came, Sam wanted to enlist, but was under war-age; a boy named Willis, who had a premature beard, left school and was said to be going to join the cavalry regiment. Sam (it was now vacation) seemed apathetic, but he disappeared and could not be found.

My father's health had been bad during the spring, and my mother prevailed on him to go to the seaside for a vacation, taking me with him. The place selected was Mount Desert, then a lovely wilderness, high up on the Maine coast. We went by train to Bangor, thence by stagecoach. After two or three delightful weeks in a farmhouse beside Frenchman's Bay, we set out homeward at the end of August.

While we were waiting for the southbound train, in Bangor, I strolled about the town by myself; most of the young fellows had enlisted, and the streets seemed empty; but, turning a corner, I saw, a block or two away, some one who looked like Willis, and I remembered that his home was in Bangor; he was talking with some one who, thought I, was either Sam Hoar or the Devil (you will recall that Sam had mysteriously disappeared from Concord). I went toward them, and I was right about Willis; but the other person had vanished.

"Sam Hoar!" said Willis, seeming astonished. "You're crazy! The last I saw of him was in Concord a month ago."

I was innocent enough to believe Willis rather than my own eyes. On the train I mentioned the incident, casually, to my father and thought no more of it. But behold! in Concord, the town was excited; Sam Hoar was still missing; the Judge was distracted, and had wired his brother, the Senator, to invoke the help of the United States Secret Service men. The boy had evidently gone to enlist. Then I remembered that I had spoken to my father, and was off to the post office. There I scribbled a note to Willis, and afterward learned that it had been delivered precisely at the moment when a detective had sauntered up and arrested Sam. Of course my father had told the Judge who had promptly wired Bangor.

But the Judge had had his lesson—the ocean of youthful determination was too much for him. Sam was allowed to enlist, under the best auspices, and a month later was at the front, exchanging shots with the enemy. Then he caught the fever, and was invalided home, almost *in articulo mortis*. But he pulled through, a gaunt but grinning skeleton, and was the hero of the Concord hour—the proud and now humble Judge grinning beside him.

The next thing we knew, Sam was placarded to deliver an address at the town hall on "What I Saw at the War." Never had even Emerson or Wendell Phillips drawn such an audience. On the platform with Sam were his father and Sanborn; Sam, sitting between them, seemed modest, almost indifferent. But his gift for wit and humor was known, and we all expected an hilarious hour. Jonas Hastings, the bootmaker, on the front bench, looked as if he somehow thought he was responsible for the whole show.

Sanborn's introduction was poor stuff—we needed a Demosthenes. Finally Sam arose, and the salvos of cheers that greeted him might have been audible in Lexington, six miles away. But Sam started droning away, not seeming to realize what was expected of him. Nothing funny in his story. Had our Sam, in losing flesh, lost also his endowment of humor, his arrows of wit? The tension gradually relaxed. At any rate here was Sam, telling his simple story.

"Our company," continued Sam, "lay flattened out one afternoon, behind a low breastwork of pine logs. Over against us, less than a hundred yards away, lay a company of Rebs, similarly protected. They were dead shots, all of 'em. If anybody raised up an inch or two, he was liable to get a bullet through his skull. The fel-

75

low next to me grunted out, "I'd give a year's growth for a chaw of tobacco!" After a minute, a man to my left whispered, "Here you are, lad," and I felt his arm reaching across my shoulders. The other boy raised up on one elbow to take the stuff—and slumped down, dead, with an ounce of lead through his skull!"

We were listening intently, for we all knew of the long and bitter struggle between the Judge and his wilful son. Four hundred pairs of eyes were fixed on Sam, who said, after a pause, "A sufficient argument—if any were needed—against indulgence in the filthy and disgusting habit of tobacco-chewing!"

For a moment there was dead silence. Then Jonas exploded in a crowlike chanticleer, and the serried benches took up the cry till the whole hall was in a roar. They shouted, they yelled, serious citizens slapped one another on the back: and, on the platform, Sanborn, master of ceremonies, suddenly emitted a screech like a soul in agony, and plunged his lofty head between his knees. But Ebenezer Rockwood led the tumult; from his mouth proceeded a bellow such as I hadn't supposed mortal lungs were capable of. The whole tradition of dignity and awe which had hitherto invested him was swept away, never to be recovered.

Sam, the perfect actor, with an expression of faint surprise and perplexity on his gaunt features, stood patiently waiting to resume his artless narrative. The keys of the town were delivered to him.

Another word on Sam Hoar. After his famous speech in Concord Town Hall "against indulgence in the filthy and disgusting habit of tobacco-chewing," we see him two years later, fully restored to health; he went up to Harvard to matriculate as "fresh-sophomore." The applicants were ranked alphabetically by the initials of their patronymics. It so happened that our Greek professor, Sophocles, was assigned to interrogate the "H's."

"Vot is your name?" thundered Sophocles, as he thundered at me some time later. Sam Hoar, standing quietly, told him. The Greek flamed with indignation.

"Vot, den, are you doing here? Gan you not spell you own name? Dis is not your blace. You belong down among de W's!"

Sam withdrew for a time. He was responsible for what he was, not for how he sounded. The error was finally corrected, and he became one of the professor's favorite pupils.

Frank Sanborn

IT HAS been the good fortune of Concord to possess a material link between the things of today and those of yesterday. Almost seventy years ago there came to Concord a tall, wiry, long-limbed young scholar with brilliant dark eyes looking keenly beneath a great shock of black hair, a quick, kindly, humorous smile brightening over his thin, fresh-hued face and finely moulded features, expressive at once of passion and self-control. He walked with long steps and with a slight bending of the shoulders, as if in modest deprecation of his own unusual stature. Such was Frank Sanborn when he first appeared on the scene in Concord, Massachusetts.

The John Brown episode had just terminated in that memorable scene where the scaffold once more became the platform of martyrdom, and none among the champions of the martyr had been more ardent and explicit than this young scholar. In him was illustrated the finest type of the pure New England strain, which took so strenuous and unfaltering a part in the process of our national regeneration. By the natural affiliation with one another of magnanimous and patriotic souls, Sanborn became united in purpose and sentiment with the high aspirations and performances of the elder great men of his time—with Garrison, and Wendell Phillips, Channing, Emerson, Alcott, and May.

He approached them in reverence, but held his own with them. His outward occupation, meanwhile, was, as we know, that of the simple and conscientious master of a country school for boys and girls, but that school became the model, often imitated but never rivaled, of advanced educational enterprise; and when after many years, the doors of the little gray schoolhouse on the village street closed forever, the name of Frank Sanborn was known and honored wherever, in New England, there was appreciation of manhood, fidelity, generosity and enlightenment.

As a small boy I was strongly prepossessed against him, and was afterward perplexed by his feminine gentleness. So I was especially interested on the two occasions when, amid the placid tides of our school, the wave foamed and struck. They were not very important occasions; but we can't always be having battles of Waterloo.

Sanborn being late in taking his chair one afternoon,

suddenly all the pupils started sneezing. Gourgas, a queer-looking chap, of French extraction, looked about with a grin. He took his hand out of his pocket and scattered an ounce or so of snuff. No harm was done or meant, but at this juncture in must step Sanborn. He halted, like the heroes of Victorian romance, drew himself up to his full height, for a moment was bewildered, and the next moment understood.

Poor Gourgas, foredoomed, broke into a guffaw. Upon him Sanborn fixed eyes more terrible than Thoreau's. "Who has done this?" he asked.

"It was me, sir!" A sin in grammar, to boot!

He was ordered into the adjoining room, and Sanborn, ruler in hand, stalked stiffly after him. Whack—whack—six times repeated. Then a pause, muffled voices: the executioner and his victim reappeared, the latter leading. He had stuck one hand in his pocket to hide the palm, reddened and swollen from his punishment. He managed also to keep up his smile—a manful gesture—and we liked him the better for his crime.

On the other occasion Sanborn struck one Bob Higginson, whose family sent him to the Concord school in hope of improving his habits, was actually expelled from the school! His weakness was bourbon—or rye! Appearing at a dance one night in anything but proper condition, and being refused a dance by one of the charming girls, he slouched away and finished the night with companions in orgies that resulted in the crashing of bricks through the schoolhouse window, and ribald outcries.

So severe a sentence as expulsion had not been anticipated. Technically just, perhaps, but was it right?

Might not a youth of high breeding, less than twenty years old, have been redeemed?

Life at Sanborn's School

MY UNCLE HORACE MANN was eager for the coeducation of the sexes, and his idea caught on enormously, broke out from top to bottom of the country, and is welcomed as a vast improvement upon our former celibate system. Whether the boys or the girls have benefited most is not for me to say. But Sanborn's school was certainly a nice place to be in.

The little red schoolhouse is, of course, historic, a sentiment as well as an institution. Sanborn took the structure ready-made, but painted it gray. It may have been forty feet long by twenty wide; it had a big stove in the center, and three walls were paneled with blackboards: the master's desk, on a low dais, being at the entrance-end. The pupils sat at desks accommodating two each, the girls on one side of the central aisle, the boys on the other: more of the latter than of the former, but enough of the former to keep the latter in order—if you know what I mean. There were all sorts and degrees, of course, but on the whole, in our mutual conduct, we were a very ladylike and gentlemanly lot. Here and there, and now and then, there might even be a pair of lovers; though taken by and large, we were mostly too young for more than transient spasms. But I may have more to say later about what we clumsily term "calf-love."

The disagreement between the South and the North came to a head about the time I entered the school, and occasioned the withdrawal of several popular young Virginians and South Carolinians. There were a few distractingly lovely girls—Grace Mitchell, Maggie Plumley, and others with whom the entire left side of the aisle was in love; but the inflammation was serious with a few only. Edward Emerson's big blue eyes would kindle into ecstasy as he bent them on Maggie, and Wilkie James, who came to us from Europe, with all the savoir-faire and graces of that region, could not preserve his poise in Grace's presence. I was out of it. In my tenth year, in Liverpool, I had been ardently in love with a Minnie Warren, who danced away from me into the Unknown, and the scene of our passion saw us no more. By the time I got to Sanborn's I was as bashful as an oyster, and shut my shell, though not unconscious of what went on around me.

Meanwhile, the menace of battle with my peers speedily faded out. Never was there a more peaceable set of youngsters; but for a time they eyed the newcomer with a certain shyness, and with more of curiosity than hostility as speculating how this foreign-bred individual might pan out. But when it appeared that, beyond a British phrase or two, and ignorance of Yankee school customs, there was nothing wrong with me, they "extended" to me (as we phrased it) a friendly hospitality, and all went merry as a school bell, or better.

Among the boys, there was Frank Stearns, who strove to introduce cricket into the school, his father, the fierce Abolitionist, providing the bats, balls, and wickets. I had never heard of baseball, which was in its infancy

81

and of the Massachusetts type. When, after a while, England seemed to favor the Southern cause, cricket was dropped, and New York baseball replaced the older game. Then there was Bill Simmons, who was the William Simmons who rowed two in the four-oar which was sent to London to row a four selected from a great Oxford crew that had beaten the English Cambridge that year. That was in 1869; the Oxford men defeated them, but not too easily. Then years later I was at Oxford and met Dr. Darbishire, who had rowed in the Oxford boat; he said, "The truth is, your men were as good as we, and rowed as well; but they wouldn't eat our food, and wouldn't drink our ale—insisted on plain cold water. The consequence was that on the day of the race every one of them was out of kilter and fitter for bed than for boating; and even at that they were a bit ahead of us at Hammersmith Bridge."

Bill, the Concord schoolboy, of course, was very different from the magnificent athlete of 1869. After the race he came to see me in Dresden, where I was finishing that engineering course.

On my daily journeys from the Wayside to school and back, I had to pass the Alcotts' house—"Apple-Slump," as Louisa dubbed it then: she had not as yet written "Little Women," but her word was already potent in Concord. After she and her delightful family had passed out, the old edifice was taken in hand by pious realtors (the term had not yet been invented, but the virus was present) and transmogrified into a sort of museum of early Americana. The building itself was renovated and given a respectable name, which I will not attempt to recall: a ghastly corpse of its dear, sim-

ple old self, scientifically embalmed and prettified, and
even parodying fanciful word-pictures in Louisa's story.

Sanborn did give me the lowest mark in declamation,
which was "14," his vivid memory to the contrary not-
withstanding, save for one Asa Collier, who was the
under-dog in everything, even in our games on the playground. But here is a last word for the despised little
Asa Collier. One day, when I was myself nearly seventy,
I stepped into the shop of a prosperous jeweler and
watchmaker, to get the correct time—and the obliging
proprietor who attended me was no other than Asa himself. We shook hands heartily, and I am sure he was far
better off in the world than I was, or ever expected
to be.

But it is full time for me to be going to school in
earnest. My forecast was gloomy. Up to that time, all I
knew about schools was what I had gathered from "Tom
Brown at Rugby," a very popular book at that time. In
fact, English public schools had then, and perhaps still
retain, many brutal features—"horsing," "fagging," and
the like; and frequent personal fights in secluded corners of the playgrounds. I had seen a good deal of
English schoolboys—unofficially, so to speak—and had
learned to use my fists; and during my Roman residence, where I became a sort of ringleader of a little
group of American boys, we once met up with a similar
crowd of juvenile Britishers, led by a tall youth who
solemnly challenged me, "in the name of the Royal
Army of England," to step forth and fight him.

Now for a chance to repeat the triumphs of 1776! I
pulled off my cap and jacket and flung them on the
ground behind me: my adversary removed his, and

neatly folded them up—a gesture of cool preparation for massacre, which did but steel my own murderous purpose. But as I made for him, with fists out, he said, in a rather pithless voice, "No hitting in the face, you know!" Whereupon, not knowing how otherwise to proceed, I caught him round the neck with both hands, and hurled him to earth with a bang. He rose slowly. "That's enough: let's shake hands and be friends," he said. My followers set up a cheer, and the challenger was thenceforward my most assiduous addict and yes-man; he was a gentlemanly boy, and I liked him. But he lacked the pertinacity of the Redcoats at Bunker Hill who kept coming until Warren's terrible sharp-shooters had used up their ammunition.

So, looking forward to meeting my fellow pupils of Sanborn's school, I took for granted a few test-battles, and all my father had to say was, "If the boys attack you, always go for the biggest one!" And he smiled airily, as if bloodshed were his middle name. For my part, I felt that I ought to be able to hold my own, for had I not been carefully instructed by English officers in smallsword and sabre, and taught to ride in the English style by retired English jockeys who had competed at Epsom? and had I not had a season or two at Huguenin's renowned gymnasium? I ought to be able to keep my end up with any boy of my size. Yes, but how about Sanborn himself, should he attempt to "horse" me, or take other liberties? When he made his introductory call at our house in the summer of 1860, I saw a very courteous and smiling ogre, six feet three in stature, whose seductive bearing did not deceive me.

Besides, I already knew his desperate character. A year

ago, with the help of his valiant sister and her broom-stick, he had vanquished two United States marshals sent to arrest him for treason, and for aiding and abet-ting John Brown's raid at Harpers Ferry. He was at this moment actually a fugitive from justice; and but for the Civil War (soon to be declared), he might have mounted the scaffold with old John!

I passed dark hours waiting for school to open. The weather was beautiful: I fished in the river, bathed in Walden Pond with the Alcott girls and the Emerson children, rode on Edward's pony and tramped the woods with Thoreau observing birds and picking up Indian arrowheads. But the September of my fate came at last. As I set forth in the early morning, my father was at the door, still with his enigmatic smile. "Remember," he called out, "always to hit the biggest!" I nodded with set teeth.

"Childe Roland to the Dark Tower came."

Frank Sanborn's little schoolhouse was surrounded by the great, fresh outdoors, and neighboring such abodes of felicity as the Alcotts' house to play and dance in; picnics at Esterbrook Farm, five miles north in the woods; bathing and skating at Walden Pond; the grand masquerade at the town hall; the regatta on the river below the old Red Bridge; a week's encampment on Monadnock Mountain—boys and girls, judiciously se-lected, but chaperoning themselves on horseback par-ties. Such diversions are quite as much characteristic of old New England as the school was, and in memory are ineffaceable.

As to the regatta—for the convenience of onlookers, it was held on a half-mile stretch of water below the

85

Red Bridge—the Oxford Henley couldn't look prettier: bright, summer frocks, and hats shading lovely faces, and boys to match. The old bridge was fluttering with flags; the great sun (as Emerson would say) shone heartily and shared the joy he brought. It was to be a rowing regatta, with a dozen contestants; but when the day came, only two faced the starter—Willie James and Sam Hoar. This was before the latter's war adventure.

At the noon hour, the spectators on the river banks and on the bridge must have numbered one hundred at least; none of us, I believe, had ever seen a rowing-race, nor did we know anything about oarsmanship. Willie James had a light roomy boat, furnished with a beautiful pair of varnished oars. Willie, inadvertently, at first took his seat on the thwart nearest the bows, and facing in that direction; but a farmer's lad admonished him from the bank, and Willie scrambled into the right position, the craft rolling alarmingly as he did so. I didn't know, till after the race was over, that Willie had never before sat in a vessel propelled by oars. He had supposed that oarsmanship came by nature.

Mr. Sanborn, up on the bridge, was now preparing to wave the starting flag. But where was Sam Hoar? Surreptitiously almost, a low, unimportant object was forging up alongside "The Oriole," Willie's elegant boat, with an old pair of pants and a sleeveless undershirt containing poor Sam. He had made the punt and oars himself, and was now foolish enough, with no better equipment, to go up against Willie. To be sure, he seemed to know how to row; but what of that?

Sanborn waved the flag, and the race was on! Had it been the Harvard-Yale race on Lake Quinsigamond, we couldn't have been more excited. Just as Willie's shiny oars touched the water, a vagrom breeze deflected the high bow of his boat, to correct which he dug one oar deep in the water. But the handle was thus driven violently into his stomach, and forced him off the thwart into the boat's bottom. A crab, first stroke!

Meanwhile Sam, pulling long and smooth, was out in front. In fact, of the race technically speaking, there is not much more to tell. By the time Willie got set again, Sam was approaching the finish. Willie, flushed and bruised, arrived at last as good-natured as ever and heartily gave his blistered hand to his rival, and laughingly apologized to the girls for making such an ass of himself. Sanborn handed Sam the silver cup amid the general acclaim, but had Sam been Edward Emerson, he would have valued more the look that Maggie Plumley gave him. But he was an odd stick in his boyhood: original, independent, shy, ironic. He had the whim to capture the school coquette, and then drop her. There was no sequel to this episode: or, like Richard Lovelace, he would say,

> I with a stronger faith embrace
> A sword, a horse, a shield.

There was variety in skating; Walden Pond, though perfect when you got there, was too remote for the crowd. The Concord River, below the Red Bridge, was close at hand, and could accommodate an army: thirty miles of ice, a quarter of a mile wide, clear way up to Lowell. The low banks of the river were overflowed in late autumn, and ice began to form soon after; it would be mixed with snow—gray, instead of the Walden black —but good enough. A big bonfire would be built and maintained near the bridge, as the rallying point; the rest of the vast sheet was open for what Theodore Winthrop called "podography." Storrow Higginson, short, square, tough, and tireless, was our best performer. But even Storrow was human; for skating backwards, once, at dazzling speed, hands clasped behind him, the heel of his left skate struck the end of a broken oar embedded in the ice. He soared aloft: at first we thought it was to be a new figure: but Storrow came down, whizzing, like an aerolite, and lit on the back of his head. There he lay, without a kick, obviously dead.

But he had on a thick woolen cap, doubled round the rim, and he owed his life to the girl who had knitted it for him, for he had just escaped a fractured skull.

Another skating episode looms before me. When Frank Stearns, also a pupil at Sanborn's school, and I were skating on the river one moonlight night, a near miracle befell us. There had been threats of a thaw; the surface of the ice had begun to soften, and in some spots was disintegrating; but out in the middle of the river it was sound enough. I started downstream, a light breeze behind me, intending to beat the record to Bailey Bridge, some ten miles below. I was soon aware that Frank Stearns was behind me, and keeping up well. I put on pace to shake him off, but he hung on. At length the low arch of the Bridge came in sight; I aimed at the central span, and looking back saw that Frank was less than twenty yards behind me.

The moon was low, and its light fell partly beneath the span, and I saw, too late, that there was no ice in a gap of thirty feet. Too late to stop, or turn: besides, my blood was up!

A matter of seconds! At the brink I perceived that a big cake of ice was floating in the gap. I was in air, crouching to avoid the timbers of the bridge overhead; an instant, and I was safe on the farther side, wheeling to warn poor Frank, whose doom seemed sure. The ice-cake which had saved me was bobbing up and down as I had left it, and it was impossible that he should hit it right. He would be carried beneath the ice by the slow stream, his body to be fished out the next spring.

But as the horror shivered through my mind, he stood safe and sound beside me, and we gazed at each other unbelieving. After a while, we hobbled to the bank and sat down on the snow to think it over. But there is no explaining miracles; we skated homeward slowly, but never so much as discussed the matter till years afterward.

Let us recall happier things! There was an acre or two of good ice close to the Red Bridge; half a dozen of us were practicing difficult feats, others looking on from the rail above. Along came somebody, an obvious tramp, ragged, and unwashed, and leaned to look, beside us. By and by he turned and said, "Pardon me, gentlemen; I used to be a bit of a skater, long ago, when I was a boy. Would one of you mind lending me his skates for a few minutes, to find out if I've forgotten?"

We glanced at him and hesitated; wasn't he the kind of loafer who would skate away on the skates and return no more? An awkward moment! Nobody spoke, and the fellow was turning away with a sorry smile, but then the Angel of the Lord whispered in my ear, and I held out to the tramp my shining "rocker" skates, given to me on Christmas. "Go ahead!" I said. He thanked me with a look, sat down, and deftly put them on. He scrambled up, and after a few trial movements, he gave us, within an area of forty yards, an exhibition of skate-magic such as Storrow himself never rivaled.

But after ten minutes, his unaccustomed ankles began to tire; he slumped down, panting, unfastened the rockers, and with a "Thanks," more worth my having than any skates, handed them back to me. Then he resumed his way westward, along the Road of Life; and I went home, and told nobody.

Our baseball, at Sanborn's, was the Massachusetts variety; the batter stood halfway between the first and fourth bases, and the player was put out, not by being touched with the ball, but by being hit with the ball on the throw. The balls were small rubber things, and hurt little if they did hit. The game had not yet been taken up by professionals; nines were actually made up of inhabitants of the places where the game was played.

Frank Sanborn's Conversation

SUCH fellowship and friendship as may subsist between a man like Frank Sanborn and a fourteen-year-old boy was begun when I had the good luck to appear as a pupil in the famous school. When I myself was almost seventy, we met again—after what an interval! That great cordial hand went out in greeting, and the smile flashed out and the eyes sparkled with the old brilliance under the wavy mass of hair, abundant as ever though now grayed by time.

No one had known Emerson both in the body and in the book better than Sanborn, and there might well be in him, in certain moods, touches of an Emersonian incarnation.

Leaving his library behind—those book-covered walls rich and inexhaustible—we entered a room full of golden reflections, as of a nook in Thoreau's woods when autumn has yellowed the elms and birches. At the hint of a tender little drawing by May Alcott the figure of the Sage of Orchard House became eloquent: and speaking of the part played by heredity in the formation of men, "Alcott inherited everything," said Sanborn, sparkling into one of his smiles. Had he said it of himself it would have been better justified, for our discursive chat, moving haphazard hither and yon, opened many a door in the rich recesses of his mind, from which stepped the figures of the vanished worthies in their habit as they lived.

From Concord we found ourselves for a moment in London, where, as Gladstone stood in the lobby of the House of Commons, his aspect from the rear had seemed like that of Ellery Channing. But not the lionlike front of him when, recalled by an attack upon him, he stood in his place on the floor of the House and rent in pieces the shrinking form of Sir Henry James. Anon Emerson appeared. "He was principled against laughter; once I resolved to test his constancy, but the story I told him, though it caused him some manifest contortions, did not actually overcome his resolution." Nevertheless, Emerson's humor was constant and deep; save for the Emerson in him he might have been a humorist, and his smile had in it the very soul of intellectual laughter.

The golden room became populous with the shapes of the departed—"the dead but sceptred sovereigns, who still rule our spirits from their urns." They moved upon a current of comment and reminiscence which was radiant with insight, sympathy, wit, and often a gleam of kindly satire. But satire had been far more frequent on Sanborn's lips in his younger times than it was in his declining years. It was a gift in him, and he had used it with the skill of a master swordsman. It was mellowed now, and rather caressed than cut. Men who reach wisdom are not harsh, but gentle. Sanborn had never ceased to grow and had therefore kept his youth. Like the noble elms which give native grandeur to Concord streets, his roots penetrated deeper, his branches spread wider, and bore fuller foliage than of yore.

But the culture derived from the past, whose perfume emanated from him at delightful intervals, as when a breeze comes from an ancient flower garden, did not prevent or diminish his active interest in current affairs. Even to note the high lights of a conversation which flowed upon its way like a careless and sun-flecked, yet profound, river, during four hours that passed for the hearer like so many minutes, would take me far beyond the limits which present conditions impose. Several volumes upon the life, activities, and thoughts of this remarkable man would hardly encompass them.

As we talked he kindled and glowed and bore with the lightsomeness of an athlete a burden of effort which might well have exhausted a man forty years his junior. His mind was athletic, catholic, and flexible, and it preserved his body from weakness and decay. I am hardly prepared to call him an optimist, but if he recognized shortcomings in man and civilization, these were powerless to depress or embitter him. In most men of his age who are not feeble or colorless, there is a certain intellectual bleakness which conveys a wintry suggestion, but I doubt if the seasons ever got beyond October with Frank Sanborn, and summer and spring were not remote from him.

After parting from him I sauntered for an hour about the familiar ways to which I had so long been a stranger —the Concord of my childhood! Contrasted with this era of change it was almost incredibly unaltered. Where new edifices had replaced the old, or had established themselves on other sites, a rare good taste had fashioned them on the old models, so that harmony was preserved. The spirit of Concord was here, and to my thinking it owed no little of its vitality to the indomitable and intrepid spirit of the wise and well-dowered personage who lived in the old cottage beside the river, who had been faithful to the great traditions of which he himself was not the least worthy and the sole surviving illustration—to Frank Sanborn.

Ralph Waldo Emerson

COMING to Ralph Waldo Emerson in my recollections, so much about this remarkable man crowds upon me that it seems futile to attempt to portray him: flesh and blood might be portrayed, but not the soul. What is best in nature cannot be put into words; moreover, like other persons of genius, he was of many moods— one man in the public nostrum, another by the fireside, in his home, another in talk with a mate, another with a child: therefore, to recall him it must needs be at length, unrestricted, as completely as words of mine can carry the significance of his unique personality to my readers.

If any man other than Emerson attempted to attain eminence in life with Emerson's bodily equipment —his physical make-up, proportions, and aspect—it would be a foregone conclusion that he must fail. He had no form or comeliness that men should heed or follow him. And yet, from youth to age—a stretch of nearly ninety years—he was the most distinguished figure in American letters and philosophy; and I doubt whether even people who knew him well realized how he really looked. Most of them would have said that he possessed beauty, and in a rare degree. His coming into a room had the magic of sunlight. In that shining aspect nobody was able to see that he was ugly, misshapen and awkward, with clumsy hands and feet, small head, contracted forehead, his nose unclassical, his face narrow and deeply seamed; that he carried his head projected somewhat forward, that he shambled in his gait. How could all this be consistent with beauty?

It is an enigma; but there have been precedents. Socrates was the homeliest and most insignificant-looking man in Athens; Mirabeau, scarred by smallpox, was aggressively ugly, but he swung the French Revolution while he lived, as the stunted Athenian did Athens. Evidently there is a hidden element in the problem—the element that we call the human soul, the existence of which many deny, and the wisest know little about.

But I am not going to try to solve mysteries or do more than suggest the Soul as the only explanation of

the truth that Emerson, in spite of the material draw-
backs and handicaps I have mentioned, was one of the
most beautiful of men with the dignity of presence and
the grace of movement of a natural king. A transfigur-
ing aura enveloped him through which he shone like
Jove or Apollo come to earth. One secret may have been
that no man had less consciousness of self than he: his
thought never stumbled over "I, Emerson." His meditations were of the Soul, and it was therefore to the Soul
that he steered the thoughts of others.

Another magic was his smile: that smile of Emerson's
was one of the high endowments not only of himself
but of those who beheld it. It was the assurance to the
world of good, truth, and faith. He smiled always with
closed eyes, so that although they were of a green-gray
hue and not large, they seemed to cast rays, dissipating
doubt and ill-will; and the eaglelike sweep of the upper
lid conveyed power and majesty. The eagle quality was
in him—the Eagle of Olympus, not rapacious but di-
vinely keen to defend Right and banish Wrong.

And if he had been indeed invisible, his voice might
have portrayed him. In conversation it was a concord
of winning sounds, courteous but affirmative; as Tennyson says of Lancelot, you were "won by the mellow
voice before you looked." When Emerson spoke in public, passing from one mood to another, commanding or
persuasive, it had the appeal of silver trumpets, and he
could gather the whole force of his argument into a cul-
minating word. How one would have liked to hear him
pronounce the lines of that short Ode or Hymn in
which he dedicated the monument at Concord Bridge

and the "shot heard round the world"! What words, what emotion, what control!

Emerson's culture was no surface adornment, but came from the marrow, so that in him nature and art were one. In his lectures, every posture and movement was moulded by his thought, so that a deaf man might have understood him. But I elaborate this portrayal in vain. He himself dispensed with elaboration. Not that he was simple, but he used himself simply. You might quote of him that verse from his poem of "The Sphinx" interpreting the riddle of Nature: "Deep love lieth under these pictures of Time: They fade in the light of their meaning sublime." Emerson was incapable of artifice, but he dwelt in the very heart of Art.

And though he attempted no disguises, you could not see through his transparency, which was like that of those crystal spheres that come from the Orient. Henry James the elder—father of the novelist and of the scholar, and a greater mind than either—relates that he once tried to make him confess himself, but was defeated because Emerson had nothing to confess, couldn't understand what his questioner was after. And James, at last, could only conclude that the Seer of Concord had never had any moral experience, any more than a virgin, or a babe unborn. There was the difference that he had knowledge: but it was theoretical. He accepted the Oracle without testing it—had none of that sort of curiosity. He disdained to challenge the verdict of the Soul by bodily experiment; at any rate abstained.

And this abstinence—defect if you like—had one singular consequence. When the poor and needy hear of a free dispensary, they flock thither for relief; and the multitude who read Emerson's wisdom in his books, or heard it in his lectures and felt need of encouragement in their own troubles, came to him for counsel. But Emerson, though benign, had no personal acquaintance with temptation, and his answer to such appeals must inevitably be, not to the individual, but to human nature. This seems very like asking for bread and receiving a stone—and no better if the stone were a diamond. Emerson might find nourishment in such food, but the sinner was not an Emerson. So there was a chill at the bottom of his charity. He could not have gone with Dante to Purgatory, but he could admire Dante.

I shall have no other criticism of Emerson to make than this: he was almost pure Intellect; but though Intellect is confident that it comprehends Love, they are really strangers. His friendship with Carlyle is historic, and the great Scot captured his imagination; but it was the Idea of him, not the presence, he valued. The higher atmospheres are cold.

His relations with Hawthorne are suggestive. He and Carlyle could sometimes see "eye to eye," but Hawthorne was adverse to specific philosophies and to their expounders. He valued mysteries and was not eager to attempt their solution. Emerson, on the other hand, could not read Hawthorne's romances, which were apt to end on a question, but he was attracted by Hawthorne himself as being a mystery which resisted even his penetration. One evening at Emerson's house there had been a colloquy between himself and several of his intimates, at which Hawthorne had remained silent, though attentive; and at last silently withdrew. Emerson, looking round with a smile, remarked, "Hawthorne rides well his horse of the night." Emerson was always on the trail of the Sphinx; Hawthorne and the Sphinx had been playmates from childhood. The two men were each unique in his own way—Emerson more on the plan of a Greek temple designed on the plans of Pheidias and Plato: Hawthorne like the Oak of Dodona, with the inscrutable symmetry of Nature. No doubt every mountain summit has its place in the sky; and the loftier the summits are, the further apart they are.

Emerson was hospitable: he kept open house on Sunday evenings, and sat at the head of the circle in the big parlor, legs crossed, and—such was their flexibility—with one foot hitched behind the other ankle. Leaning forward, elbow on one knee, he faced his guests and held converse with any, equally attentive to village tradesman or monarch of intellect; serious, but admitting occasional interludes of humor. One evening, in the midst of an earnest argument on the unreality of material things, Norah, the Irish servant, put her head in and whispered to Emerson's daughter Ellen. Ellen turned to her father and said gravely and audibly, "The butcher wants to speak to you about the mutton." Emerson uncoiled himself and rose, saying to the company, "Perhaps I would better go: perhaps the mutton may be real."

Perhaps he had thought out the expediency of modern social customs, and had formed a code of his own; but he disliked to be conspicuous, and uniformly preferred conformity to anything eccentric. For instance, though he disliked tobacco, he would sometimes puff at a cigar rather than embarrass a smoking friend.

The lyceum lecture was in its apogee in the 1860's and Concord had a dignified and commodious town hall, worthy of eloquence, each week in the season, of the great orators of the period—Edward Everett, Wendell Phillips, Henry Ward Beecher, George William Curtis, and many more. Of them all, Emerson was best liked and listened to. Not that we always understood him; his themes were lofty: but he put himself into every passage, and in the grave and flexible music of his voice, taught manhood, courage, exaltation. As we were leaving the hall one evening I overheard Prescott, the grocer, say to Jonas Hastings, the shoemaker, "Did you get that about the Oversoul?" For Jonas, like many of his trade, was a philosopher of sorts. But he shook his head: "No use wondering what he means; we know he's giving us the best there is." Yes, we were uplifted, and when, at the end of the hour, we came back to earth, saw him gather up his manuscript—which he always brought with him but never looked at—we felt that he had ceased too soon.

A Concord Town-Meeting

IN THE heat of the Civil War, a town-meeting had been summoned in Concord; it had been rumored that there were traitors in the camp, and the poison was suspected. "Copperheads," we called them, because they attack without warning. After some turbulent talk, one of the "wild-eyed" who always haunt such occasions suddenly stood up on his bench, swung his arms, and began shouting in a hoarse falsetto. Nobody knew who he was; he was not a citizen of the town, this tangled-haired, red-eyed firebrand, of the French Revolution

99

type. But what he was saying soon commanded attention. He was accusing one of our number: "Stand up,
you cowardly rascal, and confess yourself! What is he
here for among honest men? Getting points for his treason! He should be dangling on the end of a lamp-post!"

Here, somebody grabbed his coat-tails and pulled
him down; but he had said enough. News of the defeat
of the Northern armies was abroad: men of Concord
had been killed, and were being betrayed at home. The
mob-spirit is the most hideous of human manifestations,
a black and blind contagion of ferocity. Growlings and
outcries came from here and there in the hall: men
were getting up and gesticulating. But there was one
man, sitting on the bench in front of mine, who was
bending forward over his knees, his face in his hands. I
knew him; he had held honorable posts in the town:
one of his daughters, a good and pretty girl of sixteen,
was a favorite pupil in Sanborn's school. She was sobbing in sudden terror. Not without reason, for her
father was known to have been not in full accord with
the Northern cause, and was said to have uttered opinions criticizing the Abolition sentiment of New England.

The mob was all but ripe to make him an example;
it wouldn't wait for legal evidence; the South was hanging Negroes on general principles; let us give our Copperheads a taste of their own medicine!

As the uproar gathered force, I noticed a quiet figure
making his way up the aisle to the front. There was no
one on the rostrum; he went up three steps, and then
turned; and first a few and then all of us recognized
Emerson. "He's all right," muttered somebody near me;
"but he'd better look out what he says!" Emerson gazed

out over the crowd, and the face that we knew so well in peace, seemed to gather sternness; but was it for violence, or for restraint?

For what seemed a long time he neither opened his lips nor made a gesture. The confused voices gradually fell silent under that suspense, until the multitude became as one person, fronting the judge. As the moments passed, he appeared not as the Eagle of the Thunderbolts, but as Jove himself. So deep was the stillness, that I could hear the suppressed sobbing of the girl; but her father did not lift his head.

At last, in that stillness, Emerson spoke, his voice not loud, but slow, distinct, and heard in every corner of the room. He uttered one word only, three, to be precise—but the meaning was one. "Is this—Concord?" said he.

Oh, the scorn and scourge of that word! Many there present had stood with the reverent throng that heard this man, then young, speak the verses of the Hymn at the dedication of the monument to the embattled farmers, their own forefathers, who had defended Concord Bridge, and begun the revolt from tyranny. And they saw their own sons and brothers, who on the same 19th of April, eighty-six years later, had marched from Concord Green, to the music of "Yankee Doodle" on drum and fife, to save the Union, and the Law, Order, and Freedom for which those men fought and died. And in this honorable town, during the past half-century, men of high and pure repute had chosen Concord for their abode, and had aided to carry its unsullied renown, like the echo of the shots of their forefathers, round the world.

Yet at the brink of what shame was this Concord tonight? Are we to drag Law, Freedom, and Order in the dust of a mob—to inflict upon it a stain forever ineffaceable?—to show the sacrifice to have been in vain? Is this—Concord?

I hope I may be pardoned for presuming to paraphrase Emerson's pregnant word. Such were my crude reflections at the time; and I think no one present there ever forgot the tension and the crisis. Emerson still stood erect and stern on the steps above the crowd, while those below him slunk away, till only a few besides the accused and his daughter remained. Next day, the Man of the Hour was his old benign self; and I never heard any one mention the episode. Concord had escaped, and was mute.

Emerson the Lecturer

I HAVE said that Emerson's aspect and bearing were not, at first glance, prepossessing, and yet it was as edifying to look at him while he was speaking, as to hear what he spoke. I have commented on the extraordinary difference in his personal aspect which the working of his mind could effect on different occasions. If you walk down the aisle of an ancient English cathedral on an English day of alternate clouds and sunshine, and observe the stained-glass figures in the Gothic windows, you will get the simile. How dull and dingy as the shadow passes; how glorious in hue and meaning as the sun suffuses them! Emerson, the plain, commonplace Concord citizen, would enter a hall, punctual as the clock, unimpressive in his time-worn black body-coat and trousers, and plod up the aisle, stooping a little, his top-hat in one hand, his package of manuscript in the other. He would climb the half-dozen steps to the platform, lay the manuscript down on the desk, turn to deposit his hat somewhere behind him. Now he confronted us, but scarcely acknowledged the applause, having as yet done nothing to merit it. But then he would lift his head, and look, not at us, but at another audience above our heads, visible to him only; in that presence his poor form would assume state and dignity— the Eagle of Olympian Jove was before us. The grave music of his voice sounded out, measured and reined, gathering volume, filling our hush without effort. He would not descend to us, but we were uplifted toward him, understanding, for the first time, thoughts too pure and lofty for the common day. Nothing here of the oratorical tricks and subtleties of the Phillipses, Beechers, and Curtises, but the inevitable eloquence of insight, and the will to interpret.

His gestures were few and restrained. I never saw him lift his arm as high as the shoulder-level: his favorite emphasis was to bring up his clenched right hand at right angles, and then to lower it powerfully, as his voice sounded forth with the resonance of high waves breaking in calm weather on the shore. On that sea we voyaged with him, he endowing us with his vision, so that, for an hour, we were all Emersons.

No doubt there was art within. But art is a spirit which even the artist may obey but not master; a harmony superior to rules. Nothing is great that does not transcend the mortal medium through which it exists. As Emerson himself said in that early poem, "Himself

103

from God he could not free." He was transfused with that splendor which passed on from him to create our own illumination.

There was no grandiloquence in his speech. The sentences were homely, strong with the pith of daily life, for the Man stood behind every word. He was sincere as a seraph, making us desire to believe his message, even when tempted, with misgiving, to dissent. Yet all the while, in his own private person, he was as simple and natural as an old shoe. If some mischance were to occur at a lecture, as when his manuscript slipped from the high desk to the floor and was scattered far and wide among the front benches below, it was lovely to see how his concern for the inconvenience to his audience made him forget his own embarrassment. He himself hurried down, murmuring regrets and apologies, as he helped to retrieve the Winged Thoughts.

And you will recall that other episode when squeak after squeak of his newly soled shoes punctuated his every sentence, without a mitigating floor rug beneath his feet: how Emerson manned himself to quell, if not silence, them by the sovereignty of the Muse, as his address went steadily on with its froglike refrain. We applauded even more emphatically than usual: uplifted not more by the discourse itself than by the invincible valor of the lecturer.

Emerson's mind, though always poised and poignant, was not a growing mind; he began with insights and intuitions, and his after life was given to verifying and detailing them. William T. Harris, a leading educator in the 1880's, knew Emerson well, and was himself a delightful and extraordinary intellect. He compared

Emerson's essays and poems to stars in the sky—beautiful repetitions of the same thought. There are no new departures; he does not proceed from one revelation to another. His first published essay was on "Nature." It comprises his whole philosophy, and in very abstruse form; like Einstein's Theory few people understood it. Some doubted whether Emerson did: it might happen that a boy might find access to visions of Truth, obscure to the sophistications of age. At any rate, the essay provided the text on which Emerson chiefly preached afterward; and his first poem, "The Sphinx," embodies the same idea in terms even more concise and orphic.

"English Traits"—
Emerson Facing Death

THERE is one volume of Emerson's that stands out from his other works and has a lovely charm that is refreshing after so many prolonged flights into the Empyrean—in what the poet Shelley calls "the intense inane." After his first sojourn in England, Emerson was prompted to write the little book called "English Traits." A foreign country, for him, meant only the men of mark who lived in it, and the young American visitor went from one to another, seeing but undazzled, drawing out the essence of their honey, and reaching conclusions remarkably sound and just.

There is an easy dexterity and lightness of touch, too, showing that he was well within his powers, seeking rather to portray than to judge. Indeed, there is an undertone of humor in it, which Emerson seldom indulged in, except in private talks with intimate friends: a revelation of his personal charm. He looks for the best, and constantly finds it—as such seekers are likely to do. And the book gives a truer picture of the underlying spirit of England than do any of the clever satires and epigrams. It is as good today as when it was written, and no student of Emerson should forget it.

Emerson was a poet. The book of his poems is slender, and many of them are imperfect or strange; but there are verses and lines and sometimes whole compositions which reach the highest level of inspiration. Yet he avoids every subject which poets make their best hay of—love-ditties, and personalities; he attains wonderful expression, though at moments his thought may "break through language and escape," and he often deals with ideas which others would shrink from attempting. At such moments he is the greatest of poets, in the sense of being the loftiest and most exquisite; but I shall not pretend further to characterize his work.

In his last years, his external memory faded; but emotional impressions survive mental ones, and more deeply affect life. The last time I saw and spoke with Emerson was a few weeks before his death. Ellen, his eldest daughter, who had made herself his guardian in these last times, met me at the porch. She led me into the shadowy room where Emerson sat seemingly deep in reverie.

After repeated attempts to make him realize who I was, a momentary gleam of recognition came to him; he repeated my name, but his voice died away and he sank back in his mystic meditation. Ellen asked me to speak to him again. I then thought of Thomas Carlyle, from whom I had recently parted in his last phase in Chelsea, in London. The two men, though so different, had been lifelong friends. That name reached Emerson, at last.

Like a chemical solution jarred into sudden crystallization, assuming form and color, was the Sage of Concord on hearing the name of him of Chelsea. "Carlyle!" The man sat erect, and light seemed to emanate from his face. Our great Emerson had come back to earth. It was like the Prince in the Fairy Legend finding himself repossessed of youth and power. With animation and detail he began to speak of incidents of their last meeting, so many years before, with vivid emotion, as of things of yesterday. His voice renewed the tones of the ancient eloquence. I saw the high-minded young American scholar communing with the trenchant Scot, the Carlyle of laughs and frowns and prophecies and paradoxes, and the smoke of his churchwarden pipe, as they sat before the coal-fire and discussed Fate, Freewill, Foreknowledge Absolute; and, as I listened, one of them was already in his grave, and the other on the brink of his. A wonderful and touching moment!

Then, in the midst of a sentence, his voice failed. He groped for a word—it escaped him. The magic light faded and his eyes dimmed; he relaxed in his chair, murmuring to his faithful guardian, "Who is the visitor who sits yonder?"

I like to think of Emerson sitting in his library, untroubled, awaiting his summons to depart; the windows opened in the wide, pleasant, low-ceiled room in which he had worked and thought for so many years: his books surrounding him on the walls, his faithful daughter beside him.

Looking back at this distance of time, it seems to me that Emerson's intellect—his mind—had not decayed; only the grasp of the spirit upon the physical instrument had relaxed. I could imagine him standing apart, observing with amused curiosity the gropings and fumblings of the outworn and imperfect tool while he himself was awaiting the more complete response of immortality. Therefore, what was his death but a coming into his own? The things he said and wrote, and the teachings of his character, begin now to shine as never before, and to gain wider scope. To many of us, he is less a problem today than he was during his lifetime.

Henry David Thoreau

EMERSON was a sovereign optimist, seeing gold in the most unlikely places, and often seeming to find it, though it was to others invisible. And it might sometimes happen that the Golden Person, becoming for the first time aware of his value, would put on golden airs, and so confess himself to be mortal substance after all. There was a farmer in our neighborhood, a bluff, unpolished son of the soil, with a habit of putting common sense into homely language, whom Emerson ploughed up out of his native soil and celebrated as a nugget. But he soon got tarnished.

The treasure which compensated for many false

alarms was Henry David Thoreau, who was little more than a boy when Emerson first found him: for more than a year he became an actual inmate of Emerson's household. This was the impressible period of a youth's life, and Thoreau, for good or ill, never recovered from the effects of that sojourn. But he was overflowing with native vigor and flavor, so that one might almost say there was a struggle between the two men, the elder eager to impart his wealth, the younger resolved to be self-supporting and to think his own thoughts in his own way. It was an interesting situation, which some of our modern Shakespeares should adapt to the stage.

The more Emerson stuffed into Thoreau's unwilling pockets, the more did he rob him, while at the same time commanding his boundless reverence and affection. Thoreau had something individual and much worth while to say to the world, but he kept falling into an Emersonian rhythm; it even happened that his handwriting is so like Emerson's as to be easily mistaken for it. But he struggled manfully, and, after all, Emerson could never have written "Walden"; not even have looked at the theme from Thoreau's point of view.

On the other hand, it may be doubted whether Thoreau could have conceived the adventure of living alone beside Walden had it not been suggested by Emerson— not the adventure itself, but the ideas that led up to it. It is a strange complication, having several obvious morals. Thoreau died in his forties; had he lived to Emerson's age, the sequel to his story might have been yet more edifying.

Thoreau would tramp off among the pines, or sit beside Walden Pond, or roam over the Concord hills that overlook the vale, and listen to such sermons as he found there. His mood, to the outward eye, was habitually gloomy, but underneath the flesh he might be, I imagine, cheerful enough, happy at any rate. He built barriers against his fellow men for the sake of the integrity of his theories; but privately he liked them well, and would do any valiant deed for the public good.

During the Civil War, though he did not enlist, he would do what was far more distasteful to him—go to the town hall and speak for the cause. He was an abolitionist, though not of the shrieking variety: a profounder man than John Brown, and with no trace of John's pleasure in the spotlight; for, though Thoreau was congenitally egoistic, he was fierce against egotism: he revered himself as a man, but had a poor opinion of Thoreau. He was devoid of the dramatic instinct, and he hated to be observed.

Thoreau had a French streak in him, whether of the peasant or of the aristocrat I don't know; if the latter, his morality corrected it. But neither was he peasantlike. He had no social place in the world, and, the world not being to his liking as at present administered, he could not be at his ease anywhere. He was educated at Harvard, but was not happy there; he taught school for a while, but could not accommodate himself to the child mind. Land surveying, as an outdoor occupation, finally attracted him, but he must have regretted that the spaces which he thus defined were to be redeemed from wilderness; it was treason to the great mother.

Thoreau conceived the idea of building his hut beside Walden Pond, where, until the selectmen of the town interfered and dragged him to jail for taxes, he found happiness of the rather somber kind that was

possible to him; but it was never the spontaneous, un-
thinking happiness of children, nor of the faun of the
Golden Age.

He was hampered and prevented by a brain poisoned
by philosophy. He brooded over the historical past of
mankind, and over its problematic future; he could not
help perceiving that his break with civilized custom
was arbitrary and individual; he knew he was an eccentric, and not a herald of a new life. In his book
"Walden," he proves himself right, but is secretly conscious that he is nevertheless wrong. Let him live as
he would, the world would go on its way unmodified
by his rebellion. His rare faculties, his superior intellect, were wasted like a perfume in the desert.

It would not have much cheered him could he have
foreseen the present resurrection which the idle whim
of the present day has effected for him: he would have
resented being the subject of even a benevolent curiosity.

My father said of Thoreau, when the latter was
twenty-five years old: "A singular character—a young
man with much of wild, original nature still surviving
in him, but sophisticated in a way of his own. He is as
ugly as sin, long-nosed, queer-mouthed, and with un-
couth though courteous manners. But his ugliness becomes him much better than beauty. Morally and intel-
lectually, he does not seem to have found the guiding
clew." And my mother, in a letter of about the same
date, describes a skating party—her husband, Mr.
Emerson, and Mr. Thoreau. Emerson sprawled and
scrambled about in a most inelegant manner; Thoreau,
though grotesque and ungainly in figure and movement,
performed evolutions of the most intricate and surpris-

ing kind. In fact, Thoreau prided himself upon his bodily competence and accuracy, but didn't care to make himself attractive.

Thoreau had foibles, but not petty ones. He had tried to find a practical solution of the problems of existence, and he had the courage of his opinions, and would have been a martyr for their sake in the martyr era of history. To Thoreau, birds, squirrels, and hedgehogs were better behaved than men and women were; they had not lost the primeval courtesy. Oh, for a faun to pass the day with, occupied but silent! He had clever hands, and liked to be busy with them; to make things for civilized use out of raw, rustic material. But he would abhor any standardizing of his product: there ought to be a fine personal difference in all man-made things, as there is endless variety in uniformity in the infinite work of nature. The Indians, to forgather with whom he would sometimes tramp off to the Maine woods, were artificial enough for him.

His surest happiness was in discontent, and yet that was not his real happiness: he found that in forgetting himself and philosophy in the sweet intoxication of the woods, the impression spontaneously made upon his senses by the sights, sounds, and operations of natural things. He would have thought it no hardship could he have subsisted like the Prophet John in the wilderness on locusts and wild honey; and he might have left out the locusts, not disliking their taste, but because they were alive, and he had no right to destroy life. I have sometimes witnessed his pleasure in a Concord swamp in spring. Concord was celebrated for its swamps, but during several years it was Thoreau who monopolized the celebrating: the farmers would have drained them, but capital enough was lacking.

The luxuriance of the vegetation had a tropical look in spring and summer, and in autumn the reds and yellows were gorgeous. Thoreau knew all of them by heart, and in their depths, and elsewhere, on the hill-sides and in the woods, he found such a variety of un-expected flowers as to make him believe that Concord was the natural habitat of all the worth-while flowers in the world.

Perhaps if Thoreau could have been a religious fa-natic, he would have prospered better. He had no small mixture in him of the fanatic. But his faith in God was not that towering flame which the great religious re-formers have manifested; the acid of rationality was too strong in him. He was no barren atheist, but he had not fathomed the great secret, and could not preach without it. He had almost a rage for sincerity—to be as sincere as a bird, a tree, or a wolf; and the compromises and skilful locution of the church revolted him. If we cannot explain the Trinity, let us not affirm belief in it. He accepted the designation of Transcendentalist as committing him to nothing, but he did not regard him-self as a disciple of Emerson or Alcott. His virtue was that he was a misfit anywhere in human congregations; he must be himself, and nobody, not even he, knew exactly what that was.

In spite of his great love of the outdoors, Thoreau actually joined his father in the manufacture of lead pencils; and he did odd jobs for his fellow villagers, by way of earning his livelihood. And he was a diligent

113

writer of journals so that, after his death, no fewer than thirty volumes of these were discovered, and much of them printed—after his "Walden" had made him famous. But selections were made from this inchoate mass of material, and his "Works," finally were fitted into not more than ten volumes. But after all, "Walden" was enough.

Human fellowship is necessary to human beings; that was something which Thoreau never fully achieved— he thought perhaps that he didn't care for it. If he had lived longer, he might have modified his heresy—if it was heresy, and not inspiration.

Studying Nature with Thoreau

ONCE, when I was nearly seven years old, Thoreau came to the Wayside to make a survey of our land, bringing his surveying apparatus on his shoulder. I watched the short, dark, unbeautiful man with interest and followed him about, all over the place, never losing sight of a movement and never asking a question or uttering a word. The thing must have lasted a couple of hours; when we got back, Thoreau remarked to my father: "Good boy! Sharp eyes, and no tongue!" On that basis I was admitted to his friendship; a friendship or comradeship which began in 1852 and was to last until his death in 1862.

In our walks about the country, Thoreau saw everything, and would indicate the invisible to me with a silent nod of the head. The brook that skirted the foot of our meadow was another treasure-house which he discovered to me, though he was too shy to companion me there; when he had given me a glimpse of Nature in her privacy, he left me alone with her; he was not very successful in writing poetry, but he felt it. "Books in the running brooks," said Shakespeare, and I found plenty. Beside that brook on a hot August day, I would often sit, hidden from the world, thinking boy thoughts.

I learned how to snare chub, and even pickerel, with a loop made of a long-stemmed grass; dragon-flies poised like humming-birds, and insects skated zigzag on the surface, casting odd shadows on the bottom. In spring, delightful little fairy turtles would come up out of the water, with red and yellow spots on their shells—creatures no larger than a five-cent piece. Yes, Thoreau showed me things, and though it didn't aid me in the Harvard curriculum, it helped me through life.

Truly, Nature absorbed his attention, but I don't think he cared much for what is called the beauties of nature; it was her way of working, her mystery, her economy in extravagance; he delighted to trace her footsteps toward their source, and to watch her growths and developments. He liked to feel that the pursuit was endless, with mystery at both ends of it. But of color or form as valued by artists I doubt whether he took heed. He was able to say of a girl's smile, "What is it but showing me bare bones?" That may indicate a radical defect.

It may be one cause of his never having married, or shown interest in women, unless it were in Margaret Fuller, and no one could be interested in Margaret as a pleasing physical object. She was a conversationalist; the mental or emotional attrition of a group of people would warm to action, or sometimes perhaps create, her own thoughts; she would often say a "good thing" which was, in truth, but a paraphrase of what some one else had suggested. It was a sort of flattery when you saw through it, and she may have flattered Thoreau in that way; but I never was a listener to their colloquies.

A Poem by Louisa Alcott

LATE on a wintry evening a few days after Thoreau's death, sitting around the evening lamp to listen to the reading of some romance, poetry, or history, we heard a light step on the veranda, and a tap on the door. I opened the door and—no one there. Through the dark was visible the faint whiteness of the remains of the winter's snow, the dark firs standing as a hedge along the highway, and the bare boughs of the mulberry tree on the lawn. I peered to right and left: no one! But then I saw a bit of white paper lying on one of the steps and held in place by a pebble.

My father unfolded it and found a pencil-written poem signed "Louisa Alcott." The little lyric had been written to "The Genius of the Woods." My father admired it, and sent it to Fields in Boston, then the editor of the *Atlantic Monthly*. Fields liked it but he found a false rhyme:

> Spring mourns and finds herself forlorn;
> The Genius of the Woods is gone.

It was returned to Louisa for emendation, and she changed it to

> Spring mourns as for untimely frost:
> The Genius of the Woods is lost.

It just happens to be as good or better: but we were indignant at Fields, whose super-nicety might have cost us the whole lyric. Editors get that way. In the *Century* office one day I happened to remark in the presence of little Dick Gilder, then the editor, that Emerson was the greatest of American poets; he had been dead for some years at that time. Gilder was amazed and distressed. "Emerson!—why, many of his rhymes and quantities would have been inadmissible in the *Century*!" Will Carey and Buel were there; there was a silence, and the conversation was changed. Gilder himself had written and published in the magazine many pages of verse, all of it faultless in rhyme and rhythm—if not always in reason. They were afterward collected in pretty volumes; and yet do not seem to have become household words in America.

Winter in Concord

THERE were real winters in Concord: snow from two to four feet deep with drifts three times that, so that you had to "dig out." Let some philosopher interpret the spiritual meaning of that unearthly whiteness! The quicksilver in the little tin thermometer shrank down, cheered on by the applause of the children, who wanted zero at least all the time. Once in a while came a thaw, melting the surface of the snow, which then froze again, to the firmness of ice. I once skated all the way to school on it; another time, standing on top of our hill, I hailed Abbie Alcott, who was picking her way beneath, and came coasting down on her, hands in pockets, nonchalantly, while she squealed in admiration.

My sister Una and I just missed tragedy in our snow-sporting days; we had dragged the big sled up the hill, and started to slide down on it, forgetting the rail fence at the bottom. The next moment, the fence was sweeping up to meet us, and the collision would have taken our heads off; I gave a shout, and Una and I both rolled off the sled, she to the right, I to the left, coming up, though with much diminished impetus, against the lower rail. But death is constantly side-stepping children, and they don't heed it.

In the middle of one winter, I rejoiced, scratching a hole in my bedroom window-pane, to see a four-foot snow outside, drifting over the pickets of our front fence, and higher yet against the corner barn. The wind, after creating these mountains, had fallen again, and it seemed to me just the day for a walk. Una was at Dio Lewis' school in Lexington and it would be a nice gesture to call on her, and on two or three of her five or six score companions. The distance was six miles, which I commonly covered in not much over an hour.

The first half-mile was easy, the wind having swept the road nearly bare. But then came profundities; I was breast-high in it most of the time, and once stepped down into an arctic crevasse ten feet deep, daylight dwindling far above me; it was twenty minutes before I regained firm footing. Nobody else was abroad, but from doors of farmhouses would appear human figures, staring, beckoning, which I heeded not, save to wave an "Excelsior" arm, and plough onward. Hours went by—three, four, six: now the first houses of Lexington. The rough tweed sack coat and breeches that I wore were by this time frosted half an inch deep with ice—snow melted by the heat of my body, frozen again into a crackling carapace that sparkled like silver armor in the rays of the declining sun.

On the outskirts of the village I noticed a house in which dwelt, I recollected, a fellow I knew. I would go in, melt off, announce my achievement, and press on. There was a huge snowdrift outside his door, but a narrow footway had been dug through it. I knocked, the door opened, and in I blundered, with my shining honors thick upon me.

A long, narrow room was before me, densely studded on either side with women in festive attire. My friend was holding a reception! I made to retreat, but he, hospitably relentless, impelled me forward, till I found myself in a big stuffed armchair at the very end of the room, with that double rank of ladies and gentlemen between me and escape. What with my embarrassment and the heat of the room, after the frosty air outside, I began to perspire; and when my friend proposed a drink, I, thinking only of a draught of pure ice-water, gratefully acceded; he handed me a tumbler half full of a brown liquid, which might be iced tea, though its aroma was not just like that. But I downed it: I never before tasted the like; on the whole, I liked it, and emptied the glass.

Something was wrong with my eyesight! The room

began to revolve before me, the rows of guests swung and swerved, lifted and let down; at all costs I must be gone, else, some catastrophe! But how pass down along that winding aisle of petticoats? I was on my feet, plunging forward; from side to side I reeled, but the tortuousness of the route disguised, by seeming to necessitate, my ins-and-outs; a score of silken laps seemed to invite me. My hand on the latch at last—I tore it open, and dived out headlong. Blessed be zero! I was buried out of sight in that delicious snowdrift! There I lay, snuggled down into the bosom of salvation, at rest, at peace, sanity ebbing back into my brain. Well meant efforts were made to induce me to arise and return, but I snuggled only the deeper. I remember afterward my friend's remonstrance: "But you swallowed it neat, my boy! I was going to put in water: but I thought you must know . . ."

The James Brothers

HENRY JAMES had four sons, two of whom attended Frank Sanborn's school at Concord while I was there, as I have related. Christened Garth Wilkinson and Robertson, they were known in school speech as Wilkie and Bob. They were good-looking, open-hearted fellows, had been at school in Switzerland and Paris, were at home in England, spoke several languages, put on no airs, but were simple and hearty as sailors on leave. They had the best of manners and no unfortunate habits. Bob, the younger, was robust and hilarious, tough, tireless as hickory, great in the playground, not much of a scholar. Wilkie was the glass of fashion and the mould of form, but never the least clothes-conscious or la-de-da; good-natured to the marrow.

These two were perfectly delightful characters, though, of course, unknown outside their circle of personal friends. Robust Bob was full of fun and pranks and audacities, but in all a perfect gentleman in purpose and practice. He was hugely popular in the school. But Wilkie was incomparable: besides being the best dressed boy in the school, and in manners and talk the most engaging, his good humor was inexhaustible. He was of middle height, broad-shouldered and symmetrical, with a good head, well set, and a smiling countenance. Peg-top trousers were in fashion then; Wilkie's were the widest and most enviable. He was sixteen years old when he came to us, but appeared older by two or three years, being self-possessed and having the bearing of a man of the world. In the company of the ladies he was entirely at his ease, and devoted; they all loved him.

In the assault on Fort Fisher he was one of the first at the foot of the ramparts; there he got a wound in the foot, shattering some of the bones, and crippling him for life. The wound was very troublesome, and he was never afterward free from pain. He bore it stoically, concealing it as much as he could, and always cheerful, courteous, and good-humored, but with a gravity and steadiness that were new in him.

After the war he gave up civilization and fine raiment, and went down to Florida. Bob, whose youth had saved him from the war, went with him. Of course, they knew nothing of farming, but Wilkie believed he could be a farmer, and for several years the two brothers labored and went on scant rations, under that delusion. They married two native Florida girls.

But there were four James boys all together, the other two being Henry and William, whom the world was to know later. William was the eldest of the brood, and was like the Englishman of the old rhyme:

> I am an Englishman, and naked I stand here,
> A-musing in my mind what garment I shall wear.

Not that William was naked by any means, but he was capable of any profession and could decide on none. He needn't have been impatient—he was but twenty years old—but he was ready, and fretting to be off.

Fifteen years later, I was startled to run into him coming out of his lecture-room at Harvard; he was now the author of "Pragmatism"; nervous, worried, with bright troubled eyes. He was diving into the depths of his soul, but he had not found peace. He had made a mark in contemporary thought but didn't value it. A fine nature, a deep mind, but finding no rest for the sole of his foot; a modern seeker for the philosopher's stone, with an eye to see everything, but groping in the desert. He considered himself a failure, because he had found no point of friendly agreement between man's universe and man. What was the answer?

Henry James, Jr.

HENRY JAMES, two years younger than his brother William, was precocious; for a while, he didn't seem to be anything else. He was very observant, curious, meditative, conscientious—especially about the integrity of art matters. You mustn't do certain things, no matter how tempting; "The Scarlet Letter" was very powerful, but shouldn't have been written. His health was not good, but all the keener was his psychological analysis of human relations. He began by writing studious literary reviews for the *Nation* and the *Atlantic*, to which the affectionate interest of Charles Eliot Norton got him access. He couldn't have been more than twenty when he conceived a novel, to be done on strictly legitimate lines: a young man watching over the growth and development of a girl, not as her declared lover, but benevolently; page after page of unbroken comment and analysis; dialogue, he said, was not the right way to do novels. An able and precocious piece of work, completed at last in the *Atlantic,* afterward published in a volume, but never what you might call read.

But it somehow established a literary reputation, and Henry James, Jr., went on to write scores of worthy and delightful books and made himself the founder of a school. He stuck to conscience throughout, but found so many lovely rooms and gardens in that stern edifice that his public will always be glad to wander hand in hand with him through its vistas and gentle surprises.

All his life Henry James was an unremitting student of the art of fiction. This is a fact worth thinking of; there is no other living instance of it in our country. Beneath that conventional and subdued exterior he carried a radical spirit of the most remorseless and thoroughgoing stamp. There is nothing in life that he hesitated to question; nothing in art that he would not, if it seemed to him expedient, alter or transform.

Balzac in one of his short stories—one of those conceptions brief in physical dimensions but stupendous in thought and suggestion which make one of his many secure claims for immortality—the story called (in the translation) "The Hidden Masterpiece," proved that he had surveyed and comprehended the wilderness which James, years afterwards, investigated. The story is one which any artist in any branch of art ought occasionally to read and ponder.

A volume of small dimensions, containing two essays, roused more discussion than more imposing works of his. The first of the two essays is a criticism, and a very strict and severe criticism, of one of our national qualities—or absences of quality—namely, the way we use our language; a very just and valuable criticism but one which for most persons could have been made only by a vigorous effort of moral courage. For each man and woman of us must feel more or less of the sting of the lash on his or her own shoulders. Our colloquial speech is an abomination unparalleled in the annals of national language; a welter of sinful, slipshod negligence which corrupts all planes of the social community, from lowest to highest, and from which evil communications continually operating seem to become daily worse instead of better. This would be less important but for the fact that the language—the spoken language—of a people is the reflection, the picture, of the moral condition of the people themselves; it describes them, portrays them, and according as it is right or wrong, careful or heedless, pure or corrupt, damns or saves them.

It would be a good thing for us if this essay were made an indispensable part of every school and college curriculum in our country; it is the counsel and warning of a man who knew, and who had all his life specially trained himself to know, what he was talking about. Few persons are qualified to speak on the subject with more authority. His roots began at the time of our grand old orators of the Concord Lyceum lectures; in thus fearlessly speaking, Henry James has done us the best of patriotic services.

And when he so far enlarged his scope as to dally with ghostland, he became enthralling, convincing. The few tales in that vein are masterpieces. But he was a student; would experiment but not follow the lure of mere popularity.

I had the pleasure in later years of introducing Henry to the Pacific Ocean; we made the trip from Los Angeles to the coast in the trolley, and I contrived that the spectacle should burst upon him abruptly. He had fallen into talk with a fellow passenger, who was abounding in local information; when he left us I led Henry to a little elevation which I had selected to serve as the "Peak in Darien." My companion fell silent. The expanse was blue and clear. James looked for a long time without moving or speaking, taking in the scene with the appetite of a sympathetic and practised observer.

Unlike Oscar Wilde with the Atlantic, he was not disappointed; and for the rest of that day he strolled along the beach, and filled himself with its splendor and immensity.

Henry James was visiting me in Hastings, England, and we were walking on the Esplanade, with the gray waves of the English Channel thundering against the sea wall, when I asked him if he remembered telling Louisa Alcott at one of the banquets in her honor that she would meet many people who would tell her that she was a genius but that she should take his advice and not believe them! After bethinking himself seriously, he could not recall it; but he remarked, after a pause, "Well, as to her being a genius, of course, you know, she wasn't."

No one was more modest than he, or more devoted to true art; he never wrote a careless or shallow line; insight, justice, imagination and even humor filled his pages, and he never forsook his principles for the sake of popularity. He conquered his readers in critical England even sooner than he did here; and when he came into a London drawing-room, he would be surrounded by group after group of admirers, in whose presence he could not overcome a naïve embarrassment. He talked hesitatingly, as if seeking the right word; his rather prominent brown eyes, the eyes of the seer, avoided the questioning gaze, turning aside, turning to the ornaments on the ceiling; he smiled deprecatingly at all compliments, making a bon mot in self-defence;

and after half an hour, he would leave with some excuse about getting back to his books.

I used to make brief calls on him in his little room secluded from the city's uproar. He worked at a big table in a window. The table was covered with disordered sheets written on in a rather large chirography, interlined and corrected. The room was that of a serious student, from which nothing was let go without heedful revision. "Filing—can't do too much filing!" Grenville-Murray used to say to me, looking up from a page of my rough-and-ready inditing, in the old days in Dresden. James's file was as often in his hand as his pen.

When the Macmillans asked him to write the sketch of Nathaniel Hawthorne in their biographical series, he came from London to see me in Hastings, and he was in doubt and distress. We took long walks together along the undulating downs and sat on the shore under the high white cliffs. "I don't want to do it," he said again and again. "I'm not competent: and yet, if I don't, some Englishman will do it worse than I would. Your father was the greatest imaginative writer we had, and yet, I feel that his principle was wrong; there is no more powerful and beautifully written book than 'The Scarlet Letter,' and yet I believe the whole conception of it was wrong! Imagination is out of place; only the strictest realism can be right. But how can a barely known scribbler like me offer criticism on him?"

The book was written, and the shyness that pervades it, obvious to me, was interpreted by many as arrogance. It is an honest and painful piece of work, and will endure.

Henry James had a delicate, critical faculty, but the subtlety of his psychology and the extraordinary refinement of his style alienated many readers; but he has always been admired by persons of taste and discretion, and by his own fellow-writers, or some of them, who knew what difficulty they would have in doing what he had done. These persons were able to make their feeling known to the public, and the public thus became far more familiar with the fact that Henry James was an eminent novelist than they would have been if left to their unaided judgment and intelligence, for he was never popular. It is true that "Daisy Miller" was read by thousands, but that is one of his lightest works.

His first novel—the highly estimable but nearly unreadable "Watch and Ward"—was launched in the sixties, after which he put forth more than forty volumes; but he always continued to grow, and therefore to change. He remained a student all his life.

Style, manner, handling, what to leave out, what to put in, subject, color, breadth, detail, the point of view, detachment, sympathy, object, proportion, symmetry—to these and many other points he diligently applied the solvent and constructive and creative faculties of his intellect. He analyzed and amputated and pruned and expanded, resolved to run down the truth at last, or die searching for it.

At threescore, he was still as fresh and as adventurous as ever, still had the same sense of unknown seas ahead, and a Ulysses determination to "sail beyond the sunset and the baths of all the western stars," until the end.

Henry James, Sr.

INCOMPETENT for the task though I am, I want to say something of Henry James, Sr. He was the most powerful figure in the James family. Anthologies refer to him as a Sandemanian, or Glasite, or as a Swedenborgian, and a theological writer. He repudiated these titles, but supplied no substitutes for them; he was just plain Henry James. But about in mid-life, when he was happily putting finishing touches to an original interpretation of the Bible, the fruit of deep studies long continued, he became, all in a moment, the subject of an extraordinary experience.

He portrays it with tremendous force, in a book of his called "Society the Redeemed Form of Man." A demon shape was squatting in the corner of his study, raying out influences fatal to life. James's suffering was intolerable; his mental faculties were paralyzed; he never wrote another line of his essay, and never again cast an eye even of curiosity over what he had laboriously and ambitiously written. He sank into an aimless vacuity, and so remained till a woman, a friend of the family, suggested that he was probably undergoing what Swedenborg calls "vastation"; and directed him to some books which might explain better than she could what that handsome word meant.

Promptly, though with no hopeful anticipation, he got a volume and began to read, with the most eager interest. A man, perishing of some mysterious ailment, unbelievingly swallows some nostrum, and at once feels life surging through his veins—the very Elixir of Immortality! James had divined the secret of Swedenborg, and his doubts and miseries were over forever!

No other writer is so unmagnetic as Swedenborg; none is more magnetic and poignant than James; none more logical and explicit. But who understands him? Not one in ten thousand. He published half a dozen volumes of radiant and absorbing efforts to make his meaning intelligible; he paid all printers' and publishers' bills and sent gift copies to friends. They read, and once started, they couldn't help reading his pages, but the intelligent response was almost nil.

The final meaning of Swedenborg has been obscure. How could man, an abject creature of God, be endowed with self-determination? Without it, he would be but a puppet; yet with it, would he not be continuous with God—that is, God Himself? There seems to be an inherent contradiction, and moral and religious philosophy has come to grief upon it.

James's life work was to solve this enigma. Besides his "Society the Redeemed Form of Man," he wrote "Substance and Shadow," "The Secret of Swedenborg" and other books; but each book presents the same argument; he never seems to have satisfied himself with his exposition. But all the books shine with truth and sense, expressed in a style more masterly and vital than that of any other writer with whom I am acquainted.

Neither his famous son, the novelist, Henry the younger, nor the better known William, the author of the pragmatic philosophy, makes any approach to the power, charm, and tremendous earnestness of the father's works. A rich sense of humor underlies them all, not of course expressed in jest or fancy, but belonging to a mind comprehending its theme in all its aspects and relations, and therefore handling it with lightness as well as power.

Once introduced to these books, one rereads them again and again, with ever-increasing delight and edification. Whether they are "Swedenborg" has been questioned; they derive from him, but have an independence of their own. Neither Henry James nor William was able to elucidate them, though the latter did his best to explore their inwardness, and in his biographical essay on his father he attempts to summarize his conclusions, while admitting that they are inadequate. Members of the orthodox Swedenborgian Church —the Church of the New Jerusalem, as they call themselves—do not, I believe, fully accept James's doctrines.

James the elder, as I knew him, was broad-shouldered and vital, though partly crippled by lameness; with a gray beard, and eyes whose power and penetration spectacles could not disguise. He was as cheery as a demigod, his cheeks mantling with mirth; masculine, terrible, gentle, ebullient with humor. He towered over other men, yet was self-effacing; loved but laughed at such men as Carlyle and Emerson, Napoleon and Confucius, and all and any Gogs and Magogs of our worship: but he loved and reverenced all men, down to the least and lowest, because all were conduits, if only to an infinitesimal degree, of the Perfect Good and

PART THREE

Concord Days
and Harvard

A Mask Ball

A MASK BALL at the Town Hall in my boyhood in
Concord attracted me, and I decided to go as the great
Duke of Buckingham—the Shakespearean one, whose
head Richard III, in the Colley Cibber version, orders
to be struck off. "So much of Buckingham!" says the
hunchback devil, rubbing his hands. Shakespeare hadn't
thought of that—a favorite line with actors. I had seen
Booth as Richard; and had also heard Wilkie James
declaim the farewell speech of the beheaded one: "An',
if he eveh speak of Bookingham, prah tell him that ya
mett 'im half in Heav'n." This was Wilkie's dramatic
style, which we all admired. I couldn't rival him, but I
could represent the Duke at the masquerade—if only I
could get the velvet and silken attire, and the plumed
hat, which he wore on the stage.

My mother and sisters could make anything in reason
for any occasion, but the Buckingham apparel was beyond them. In the emergency, our family friend James
T. Fields suggested applying to William Warren. But
Warren, leading high-comedian of the period, could
never have acted Buckingham! No, but actors have a
fad of collecting clothes merely for the atmosphere, as
some men collect books, not to read them, but for the
companionship of the backs on the shelf. So Fields

presented me to the incomparable Warren. For the first time in my life I was in the private home of an actor.

Great comedians knew more of the art and science of acting than any others did. The playwright blocked out a part; Warren made it into a human being. The great Sothern, father of Edward H. Sothern, possessed this gift in the highest degree. He built Dundreary behind the footlights in sight of the audience, fitting gag into gag until the figure stood complete before us. Gags are illegitimate, and die with the originators; but with a genius like the elder Sothern they are the life of the play; illegitimate offspring are sometimes that way.

Warren, then, having ascertained my needs, conducted me to his chamber of costumes, his old dressing-gown flopping at his heels. Long lines of them depended from hooks—lifeless sheaths of art's mockeries of life. Muttering to himself, as memory (doubtless) recalled trials and triumphs which they were associated with in the past, at last he lifted out a splendid garb, and holding it at arm's length, sized me up with a glance. "I fancy we're about the same height and make," he said. Then he led me to a tall and wide mirror, and put the plumed hat on my head while I stood there. "There, sir; his Grace himself couldn't look better!" It was a famous masquerade.

In England, in my childhood, I was given a six-foot-square plot of ground for my own garden; good loam, but with pebbles in it, which I was told to take out. Out they came, therefore, but there were others beneath them, and by and by my garden was a cavity. I planted flowers but pulled them up occasionally to see how they grew; seeds of weeds fell from the air; garden snails visited the place, interesting in themselves, but bad company; I decided not to be a gardener, though I had a good rose or two.

A spiritual symbol; every boy's soul is a garden. From the age of twelve on, it should be inspected, weeds and poisonous toadstools taken out, good things planted. Religion and morals, sown with judgment and moderation, are all right; but as I look back, I think good poetry, for week-days as well as Sundays, is best.

It fits every mood and need with the fragrance of wisdom and beauty. Great poets, and some less than great, have thought it out, or felt it, and have the gift to put it into lovely and poignant words, which stay in the memory, and correct and purify your own crude impulses and notions. Shakespeare, Milton, Tennyson are the master gardeners. A boy, familiar with what in them belongs to a boy, has access to a life higher than his natural one, which puts to shame unworthy things. Beneficent magicians, they give light and grace and courage to his steps; arduous sometimes, but wholesome. Good poetry in your mind girds your loins with strength, and picks you up when you stumble.

In love—and boys are always in love—good poets do them yeoman service, though here, too, is the danger. Swinburne's music is alluring but mischievous; Lovelace's word is better: "I could not love thee, dear, so much, loved I not honor more!" But clean boys are good critics, and prefer the smell of roses to patchouli: roses, or spring grass, or beefsteak and onions at dinner-time. Toadstools wear pretty colors but smell rotten, and boys learn to distrust color and believe in good smells.

Shakespeare, Spenser, Milton, and Tennyson were

the poets I knew first and best in my childhood and boyhood: Spenser's "Faerie Queene," Shakespeare's songs, Milton's "Allegro" and "Penseroso," passages of "Comus" and "Paradise Lost"; the Sonnets I discovered later. For outdoor moods I stuck to Walter Scott, whether in verse or prose. But Tennyson was the nineteenth century poet and shibboleth; who knew not him would be himself unknown. He seemed created and creating especially for our needs, and even the first flights of his "Idylls" were welcome. The enchantment of his later muse seemed not always up to the mark.

Dio Lewis: Introducing
a New Hygiene

ONE autumn day there came into our village of Concord a shortish and chunky but not obese man, with masses of yellow hair curling up over his head, and a thick yellow beard screening his necktie, the more since he carried his head erect with the chin down, like a horse bridled. His chest was out, his abdomen severely indrawn. He took short steps and wore an air of importance; when he stood, his knees were straight.

He was somebody; in fact, we soon learned that he was Dr. Dio Lewis, instructor and trainer in the new hygiene and gymnastics. His manner of address was deferential to the Upper Ten, like Emerson and Judge Hoar; gracious in degrees to the commoner sort, polished to ladies, fatherly to the girls. To the boys his

bearing was kindly but critical; his elocution was correct and confident. He sent in his card to our best
houses and to Mr. Sanborn, and soon he hired the Town
Hall for an evening and distributed circulars. He was,
it appeared, nationally known; his mission, to do good
to the mind through judicious cultivation of the body.
He would explain himself at greater length on Saturday evening; admission free.

He had a full audience: Emerson and our other Tall
Men in front, the girls and boys of Sanborn's school
close up, Sanborn himself at full length on the platform, to introduce the lecturer and to give tone to the
proceedings. He had a wife, who assisted in the handling of the young ladies, for the Doctor was rigorous in
observance of the proprieties. He used her in his dem-
onstrations as a sort of chopping-block: thumping her
chest, flexing her joints, posing and disposing her; she
accommodating herself with smiling good humor. The
wooden jointed models that artists use were she, before
transubstantiation.

The Doctor stated in a full and agreeable voice that
his method was free-hand, no heavyweight apparatus,
simple but varied extension movements. Grace, control,
rhythm. No hard, unsightly muscles: symmetry, flexibility, smoothness, the Greek ideal.

He produced two iron dumb-bells and asked for two
of the strongest of the young gentlemen present to come
up and place them on the scales. He smiled down at us,
and Bill Simmons and I, nudged by our companions,
bashfully climbed onto the platform, and Bill stooped
and laid hands on one of the dumb-bells; but it seemed
to have been riveted to the floor, and budged not: after
a few moments' whole-souled effort, he turned to me,

who was prepared to tackle the other dumb-bell. "Some trick about this, I guess," he muttered *sotto voce*, fetching his breath.

Now, during my residence abroad, I had attended a gymnasium, and what with bars, clubs, rings and weights had gained some proficiency; my father had imported one of the combination exercising machines to this country, and it had been set up in our barn, where I had practiced on it: so, though I had never seen dumb-bells as big as these, I was confident I could best them. I bent to the task, grasped the handle firmly, and putting a fury of strength into the struggle, tugged amain. Nothing happened, except that I thought I had stirred the thing about a quarter of an inch. "It's too heavy, that's all," I said to Bill.

The doctor smiled and stroked his beard; and I have never since then witnessed anything in this kind more surprising. Standing between the bells, and grasping one in each hand, he slowly "curled" them to his shoulder, lifted himself erect, and steadily sent them aloft to the full reach of his arms over his head. Steadily he let them down again, and deposited them lightly on the floor. "And I merely wish to assure you that the ability to do this is due, not to heavyweight practice, but to the free and facile movements I have described."

There was no answer to this argument, except a burst of cordial handclapping from everybody. After a year or two Dr. Dio Lewis was able to purchase a large old hotel in Lexington and remodeled it into a school for young ladies. More than three hundred of them attended, drawn from all parts of the Union. The most striking innovation was the costumes; it was half a century too soon for the modern bathing-dress style, but the girls wore blouses and Zouave breeches to the knee, and then a charming revelation of stockings. In this guise the girls would tramp all over the neighboring country, educating the inhabitants as they went.

After years of prosperity, during a summer vacation, the school caught fire and blazed up like an old tinder-box. All the girls had gone home, and the local firemen were at a picnic. My sister Una was visiting a friend in the village, and came to the Doctor's assistance; but what could be done on a scorching day in August, with no water except in the ice cooler? Before the village folk could assemble for the spectacle, it was over; nothing left but embers and a whiff of smoke. Two years afterward he appeared in Sag Harbor, Long Island, and gave a lecture: he was as brisk as ever; ten years later he was in Philadelphia, still prosperous and full of vigor; his hair and beard were touched with gray, but he declared that he expected to live to a hundred. But he got blood-poisoning and was dead in a week. You never can tell!

Ephraim W. Gurney

THE excellent Sanborn had the job not only of teaching me things every boy ought to know, but of preparing me for college—not quite the same thing. I have a notion that what I got from him was less useful to me in later life than what I derived from intercourse

with my fellow pupils, and from the natural enlightenment of the three years from my fourteenth to my
seventeenth. It was at the latter age that normal New
England boys were supposed to be ripe for matriculation. I looked forward to the examinations with hope
and fear; for Harvard seemed to forebode an ideal,
Heavenlike, or at least Paradisical. But the matriculation! The very word intimidated, and to this day I'm
not sure that I know just what it means. Examination,
yes; but matriculation? Is it just a scare-mask assumed
by the faculty to make the applicant forget all he knows?
Things are of course different now; but in 1863, the
scare was held to be an essential feature of the regimen.

Mr. Sanborn must have shared my misgivings as to
that matriculation, for a few months before the examinations, he got the consent of a Harvard tutor to undertake my ultimate polishing-up. This gentleman, afterward a professor and eminent among scholars, was
Ephraim W. Gurney; at Harvard he chose to teach
Latin. He was of middle height, with brown hair over
his forehead and a short full brown beard; kindly eyes,
full of perceptions and responses; a kindly humor en-
riching his thoughts and his words; who knew the world
and was not embittered. To him, my father was the
greatest of American imaginative writers; they had
never met, but he received me in the rays of that genius.
From our first hour together we were friends; and every
hour, to me, was growth and pleasure. I had nothing
but a boy's affection to give him in return; but he would
admit no inequalities in friendship.

The difference I felt between him and poor Sanborn
was as between a Rasselas' Happy Valley, with rivers,
woods and far-away mountains—a gracious region of

pastures and herds, mansions bosomed high in tufted trees, winding roads and flowered lanes and old-time hedges, the atmosphere of a hundred centuries of repose and history—and a new-made town-lot with a white painted frame house, overlooking the little grassplot, a polished brass knocker on the door, and a neat flower-bed. Learning, with Gurney, was delightful and endless; with Sanborn, an uneasy training for specific and transient ends; Sanborn was punctual and conscientious, bound between today and yesterday; with Gurney I seemed to stroll with Horace and Vergil, to hear afar the ocean thunders of Homer, to observe the processes of the constellations: to discern a philosophy, "not harsh and crabbed, as dull fools suppose, but musical as is Apollo's lute"—the tintinnabulation of a school bell against the glorious reverberations of a minster organ.

This is not to belittle or abuse Sanborn—a man much more useful in a modern community than Gurney. If one must wriggle through existence without dislocations or abrasions, one must draw in the tentacles of the soul and bunt one's way as in football. But the beautiful horizons and the high mountains remain after the football scrimmage is over.

I came upon a letter lately, that I had written to my mother at the time I went up for my first examinations at Harvard, in 1863. I quote a very telling sentence or two, which amuses me greatly now, after more than sixty years have passed.

"I am very well although I feel somewhat anxious about the examinations. If I get in, it will be by the skin of my teeth. I shall be very savage if I don't . . . I shant see you again till I have either triumphed or died in the attempt."

143

My father had not taken high rank in Bowdoin scholarship, but he learned human association, and friendships. I don't think he wanted me to achieve high honors in the classroom, though neither did he, probably, contemplate my distinction in athletics. He wanted me to measure myself against my fellows, as a forecast of what I might become in after life. But we never conversed on that subject. Our dialogues always had a humorous tinge, and he affected to regard my chances of "getting in" as tenuous: "I hope you will, but you probably won't," was his last laughing word to me as I set out for Cambridge on the adventure. He may have intended to relieve me of my nervous anxiety; he may have known—for he knew me—that his doubt would kindle my best efforts. It happened that I was prevented from bringing news of my success to the Wayside; but my mother told me afterward that he had been deeply pleased.

In the main it was Gurney's doing, more than I then realized. My examination papers must have been pretty ragged, leading off with the Latin, but Gurney knew that I was better in Latin than at anything else, and that my botching was due to nervousness; he motioned me to stay after the others had gone out, and he gave me a sharp talking-to—the only scolding I ever had from him. I guess it saved my academic parturition. I muddled through, with a "condition" in mathematics, which was never retrieved, but impeded me like a tight shoe during all my Harvard years. But oh, what a good time I had!

The idea of College, as I looked forward to it, filled me with a tremulous but pleasing awe, very different from my emotions before school days. My room was destined to be on the southeast corner of Hollis, ground floor; and my chum, Johnnie Jackson, son of Dr. Jackson, nephew therefore of Mrs. Emerson.

Harvard College (or University) would then number about four hundred undergraduates, all told, including the Law School and the Lawrence Scientific School; the class which I called mine, due to graduate in the year 1867, mustered about sixty off and on. We boys figured the college to be three miles from Parker's Hotel on School Street, opposite the old stone church and the burial ground, and north from the Old Corner Book Store on Washington: a short and narrow way, but of renown. Parker's, along with the Boston Theatre and Morris Brothers', Pell and Trowbridge's Negro Minstrel House, was Boston to most Harvard students. And I saw there, one evening, the wild celebration of victory in the Civil War; and not long after, the grim mourning at the assassination of Lincoln.

Cambridge in 1860

THE freshman class of '71, which entered Harvard just as I was leaving, was the largest on record—nearly eighty! and prophets were declaring that the time would come when there would be a full hundred men to a class or even more. But nobody was bold or imaginative enough to foretell a coed. There were girls enough about, but they were the Cambridge young ladies, lovely in their hoop-skirts and wide hats, but remote and intimidating; your love of them was as that of the moth for the star.

Cambridge, in my memory's eye of 1860, is a small comely town on the banks of the Charles River, three miles by horse car from Boston, or you could walk it if you were in a hurry; and people had legs in the sixties. It was a nice walk, with the river just across the meadows; and you saved the carfare, three cents, quite an item in one's expense account.

Starting from the previously mentioned Parker's, that collegiate Mecca, you arrive in Harvard Square, an irregular space, the junction of three streets; and you see before you a time-honored wooden pump, and just beyond it a flight of granite steps leading into the town post office. Farther northward the country road would take you past a handsome mansion on your right, with the poet Longfellow perhaps emerging from the doorway, smiling, smartly clad, and very good-looking in his early fifties. Still keeping onward you would see Lowell's house withdrawn behind trees; but Lowell is a good deal of a hermit, and does not encourage callers.

The wooden-fenced inclosure which contains the Harvard College dormitories and other buildings now lies east of north across the way. You have pleasant glimpses of ancient brick buildings and tall wide-branching elms: and in and out of the gateposts, and entering or leaving the building, and passing from sun to shadow beneath the trees, are numbers of nice young fellows, in wide peg-top trousers, soft hats or caps, with once in a while a "beaver" sending forth black gleams. They come and go with hands in pockets, or playing with a cane, well-mannered, agreeable youths, these grandfathers of the boys of 1936.

Four or five ancient brick buildings faced the white limestone edifice, with a flight of steps at each end, containing the recitation rooms, and the awful chamber in which the faculty meetings were held. Back of that to the left was the college chapel, and still farther eastward the little circular building with the conical roof, fitted up within as a gymnasium. Northward across the road was a triangular piece of vacant ground, the Delta, where we played baseball, and football—when that was permitted. Harvard College—we didn't speak of a University—was a lovely place, just big enough and just small enough to be loved, and it was the abode of felicity, four hundred strong. Everybody knew everybody else, for one thing, and no unimportant thing either.

On the evening after the examinations for entrance, every applicant must go up to the Faculty-room to hear his fate. A group of us gradually formed at the foot of the steps to welcome or condole with those descending, after victory or defeat. Another life symbol: but we were more demonstrative then; in youth, consequences don't seem final; even death is a new beginning, doubt or deny though one may.

I was on the victor side, as I have said, but I shall never forget the heart-trying day—I sat with one examination paper after another before me, and beside me and up and down the long tables sat my companions in mental dissection, serious and intent. The list of questions was neatly printed, and at first glance entirely unintelligible. I knew nothing. I was lost! Time was passing too, fast and faster. Not before nor since have I known how little I knew. At last I would make shift to scribble down something; but oh, those jaws of ignorance, how wide they yawned!

My depression as the day proceeded was grim and dark, when all at once Professor Gurney, who had coached me for the trial, called me to him and said, "Stop being scared! Stop it! You know more than enough, more than most of the boys here. Thaw out your wits, my boy; be yourself!" Back I went to my task, with a desperate and reckless courage; and the thought of Gurney's confidence carried me through.

The moment I had finished my last sheet, I was serene and clear. I was sure I had failed, but had the thing to be done over again, I could have won a complete success. Yes, I knew it all now: but it was too late. I could have answered even the mathematical questions.

How I mounted those interminable steps to hear my fate from the Faculty, I never knew, but I rejoined my companions like a balloon of optimism, hardly keeping my feet on earth: all was well!

First Days of a Freshman

ON THE evening after the examinations for entrance, having come out victorious, three of us, Clem Fay, Eliot Clarke, and myself, had an oyster stew; then in the cool summer twilight, we strolled away on the Brighton road toward the setting moon, light-hearted and romantic. "Collegians!" we said to one another, gripping hands. We were in a high and happy mood. After some leisurely miles we came, in the luminous dusk, to a church; Clem said: "I play the organ in there sometimes. Let's go in—I know where they keep the key." And we entered the sacred interior. We felt reverent, stepping softly, hats off. Clem played a few low

JULIAN HAWTHORNE
at seventeen when he entered Harvard

bars; the last of the moonlight came through a western window, and touched his red head: I had never felt more religious, thinking of God, and matriculation, and my coming years in Harvard and in the world. I have never forgotten that impression, and I record the episode here, as perhaps typical of home-grown New England youth in the year 1863. It would seem incredible today—a naïve example of unenlightened superstition.

We strolled back to Harvard, serious and taciturn, but happy, ministered unto by angels.

Prayers at six-fifteen every morning, old Peabo in the pulpit, rising, closing his eyes, and beginning, "O Thou," ending at six-thirty. If you were not in your seat on the dot, the spotter in your pew marked you for a demerit. Tardy worshipers could have been seen streaking chapelward across the Green, buttoning their trousers or collars, or hiding all deficiencies under an overcoat. "Old Peabo" was Dr. Andrew Peabody, a relative of my own on my mother's side, good as refined gold, very nearsighted. Once (the legend runs), crossing the street in front of the post office, trying to read a letter held close to his right eye, he ran into the town pump, grasped the handle and shook it—"I beg your pardon!" I don't guarantee this; it was "like him," that's all. But, speaking of the post office, I am reminded of a letter handed out to me in my freshman year, legibly addressed "Julian Hawthorne, Freshman, Harvard College."

It was one of the chief aims in life of freshmen of that era to hide their freshmanship like a murder secret, pretending to be a soph, junior or even senior. I felt like a balloon punctured, and tore the envelope into tiny bits; but the letter turned out to be from my beloved and honored Aunt Lizzie Peabody, who never intended harm to any mortal creature.

After prayers, breakfast; usually a dozen or more of us would be fed thrice daily in the private dining-room of some good lady who thus made her domestic ends meet; simple, hearty, abundant meals, they were. Thence to our rooms, which had meanwhile been cleaned and beds made by the slavey, a deplorable replica of Dickens's Mrs. Gamp, who evidently needed a job, but looked and smelt more likely to contaminate than to purify whatever she touched; but the Faculty, doubtless, knew or had been warned of the perils of pretty housemaids, and stampeded to the other extreme. Had we been versed in eighteenth century literature, we might have quoted,

> Perhaps it was right to dissemble your love,
> But why did you kick me down stairs?

After these ladies had taken their pails and departed, we settled down to study for the first recitation at nine o'clock.

After a day or two of seraphic bliss—our two first—before the class of '67 had attained full self-consciousness, the whole threescore of us found ourselves massed on the Delta for our first trial of strength with the hated sophomores of '66. The pretext was football. And yonder opposite, a dozen yards away, stood in serried ranks the drilled and confident army of our foes. Somebody kicked the ball, unlike the oval missile of today. The rules of the game were simple: get the ball over the other fellow's goal-line, and knock down every man you meet. It was already twilight; as Scott says,

Then foot, and point, and eye opposed,
In dubious strife they darkly closed.

In that hour, like Tennyson's Ulysses, each of us drank delight of battle with our peers, far on the ringing plain of Harvard Delta. I happened to be in the front rank of our advance, and found myself front to front with a broad-shouldered, ruddy-faced young fellow, at whom I struck heartily. Down he went, with an expression of great surprise on his handsome visage, and it wasn't until days afterward that I learned that he was accounted one of the most redoubtable of the sophomores—Ned Perkins, no less! By that one chance blow I achieved renown which clung to me all through college. Such is life! Ned and I became great friends, and he never realized that he could have licked me any day.

Alarms and excursions. With more than a hundred warriors on the field each fighting independently, with all order abandoned and darkness falling, description becomes difficult. The field was strewn with fragments of clothing, and with not a few bodies. Then a whistle blew, and the rumor spread that the minions of the Faculty were upon us. In a few minutes the class of '67 was left master of the field, as the sophomores were already known personally to the Faculty and we were newcomers. So we justly claimed the victory. It was the last battle of its kind at Harvard.

Football—
Initiation into Delta Kappa Epsilon

IT HAD been the custom for years past, at the time of my freshman year at Harvard, to decree a football match at the beginning of the term between the new-come freshmen and the sophomores, fresh from their own penitential year, and eager to requite upon their hereditary foes the indignities from which they had suffered. All the odds were of course on them; they were a year stronger, and they knew one another, whereas the freshmen knew nothing, themselves included.

We met on the Delta about four o'clock on the September afternoon; and for "gallery" we had most of the other two classes. The goal posts were set up at the east end of the field; the ball was spherical, made of rubber, and inflated through a little key or tube fitting into a corresponding orifice, blown into by the best lungs available. It was liable to leak during a lively game, and must be refilled, while the cohorts waited. The rules of the game were simple, and I recount them to the enlightenment of posterity. The entire class on each side was supposed to participate. There was only one goal, and after the ball had been driven past it, the foemen changed sides. Therefore one party charged, while the other defended; and the best two out of three won. That was simple; but with fifty to sixty players on a side, there might be complications. And in practice it came down to a free fight between the sophs and the freshies—not so much simple as primitive. The ball was generally lost early in the game, and nobody missed it, till somebody chanced to stumble upon it, and carry it past the posts. Then somebody blew a whistle, and we faced the other way.

If this confuses you, it the better describes the state of mind of the contestants. There were no uniforms, but foreseeing persons wore their worst clothes. It did not take long for the opposing ranks to get thoroughly mixed; the practice was, when you saw a head, hit it. Suddenly we saw a figure in a silk hat and black body-coat standing with uplifted hand, dominant against the carnage. It was none other than George Washington Copp Noble, a member of the Faculty, with his English whiskers (though he was a born Yankee), and the handsomest man in the University.

When the Faculty met, the next day, it was announced on the ukase of President Thomas Hill that the annual historic football game between the two classes was hereby abolished forevermore: regrettable scenes of disorder and violence had occurred, unworthy of the fair name of Harvard; and this was the end.

The week following the decision, as the Faculty were gathered for the regular evening consultation, and the peace of evening reigned in the college yard, a terrifying crash was heard, the window opposite the consultation-table shivered into splinters, and a paving-stone whizzed across the room, missed the President's head by inches, and smashed a glazed photograph of a distinguished alumnus on the opposite wall.

The chemistry tutor branded Horatio Curtis as the guilty one—a mighty giant, prone to occasional sprees during which, in mere happy play, he might inadvertently commit annihilation on the spur of the moment. He couldn't be convicted of the act, but, as Walter Scott says of the Douglas in "The Lady of the Lake," "Such blow no other hand could deal"; and Horatio goes down in history as the culprit.

On the night of May 18, 1864, I was initiated into a college secret society—a couple of hours of grotesque and good-humored rodomontade and horseplay, in which I coöperated as in a kind of pleasant nightmare, confident, even when branded with a red-hot iron or doused head-over-heels in boiling oil, that it would come out all right. The neophyte is effectively blindfolded during the proceedings; and at last, still sightless, I was led down flights of steps into a silent crypt, and helped into a coffin, where I was to lie until the Resurrection. By and by a friendly demon came and conversed with me sitting on the edge of the coffin. The voice of this Damned Soul reminded me of the deep tones of the gigantic Horatio Curtis, with whom, while still on earth and in the Harvard gymnasium, I had talked as man with man. After a while he went away and I lay in peace: until a bevy of roistering friends arrived, hoisted me out, hurried me up the steps, snatched off bandages and lo! I was in a brightly lighted room filled with jolly fellows who were shaking hands with me, giving me the "grip," and leading me to a large bowl brimming with claret punch. The rest of the evening (though it was about two in the morning by that time) was passed in dance and Provençal song and sunburnt mirth, or in relaxations of that kind.

Charley Gage, also among the initiates, was a poet. I saw him trying to light his cigar at an extinguished gas jet, and as I had restricted myself to a single glass of the punch—being in training for the crew—it fell to me to conduct him home before dawn, while all the mighty heart of Harvard was lying still. "Dekes, old boy!" he murmured, as he tumbled into bed.

I managed to make my pew for Peabo's prayer, and the mild and sunny day flowed on.

Death of Nathaniel Hawthorne

EARLY in the afternoon of the day following my initiation into the Delta Kappa Epsilon, at Harvard, Frank Stearns and I were leisurely strolling down the street in the direction of the Washington Elm, which still spread abroad its majestic but decrepit boughs at that epoch, when we were stopped by two classmates with very grave faces. One of them drew me apart, and said, "I have bad news for you, Hawthorne—very bad!" and stammered and seemed embarrassed.

The mind travels, under certain stimuli, from Dan to Beersheba in an instant. I knew, in the drawing of a breath, that I was to hear tidings of death. Whose?

"My mother?"

"Your father."

I turned aside and leaned against the fence, an iron

155

picket-fence enclosing some one's front yard. After the two classmates had gone, Frank began to say something to me, but I made him a sign not to speak. Presently we sat down on the stone coping, and I slowly began to think.

Why had my first fear been not for my father but for my mother? She had always been, as I knew her, a healthy woman. On the other hand, it had never occurred to me as possible that my father could die. He had been frail of late, to be sure, but there seemed to be nothing specific the matter with him; only he had lost flesh and looked pale. But my feeling about him from my childhood had been that he was invincible over all mortal ills, and that he would recover his strength and activity. My college residence had been the first interruption in our daily close companionship.

On a Sunday in the middle of May, in my first college year, 1864, I walked from Harvard to Concord for a look at the home folks. I had been rereading, recently, Longfellow's poem, "Evangeline," and had been impressed anew with the eloquence and pathos of the passage describing the death of Gabriel, Evangeline's long-sought lover. My father and I were sitting alone in the little library at the Wayside; the book lay on the table, and I picked it up and read the page or two aloud to him. I couldn't keep the emotion out of my voice, partly because of a thought passing through my mind, unexpectedly and for the first time, "What if my father were to die!" After the reading, to which he had listened attentively, with a look of reverie on his face, we both sat silent, till I got up to begin my walk back to Harvard. And that was the last time I saw my father.

Thus it was that just as my father passed from this earth, I was lying in a coffin during my initiation into the Delta Kappa Epsilon. My life had been so wholly one with my father and mother that I couldn't comprehend being severed from either of them. The intimacy of mother and child is more constant, though not deeper than the other: so, when the stroke of loss suddenly fell, fatal and irrevocable, it was to her that my instinct first pointed.

But my father! My little world tumbled about my ears. Trifling details stood out, meaningless, stones in the desert. Harvard, which had bulked so large, faded like a mirage. Finally the thought of Gurney began to emerge, and soon I found myself before his door, and I became aware that poor Frank had followed me. I found Gurney in his room; I remember nothing of what either of us said, but his sympathy was balm. Later a message came from Fields, asking me to go with him to Concord. Frank recalled a remark of Gurney's: "Thackeray last year; and now the much greater loss of Hawthorne!"

I parted from Frank Stearns at the Old Corner Bookstore, and Fields and I took the train to Concord. Pierce had already come down from Plymouth with my father's body. In the train, a man in the seat in front, reading a newspaper, said to the man beside him, "Hullo! Hawthorne's dead!" Fields leaned forward and spoke in the man's ear, and the man half glanced over his shoulder and was silent; but I wouldn't have minded. By and by we were in Concord and driving up to the Wayside, and then, for a space, Fields disappeared and I was with my mother and sisters.

Women manage themselves, in these matters, more naturally and better than men do. Pierce had already been at the house, and gone. While Fields was with my mother in the library, Una and Rose and I went out into the orchard, and they told me little incidents, as we walked up and down. I knew that it was my duty to be manly and comforting, that I must give up Harvard and stay at home and take care of things; but I felt my incompetence as if I had lost my arms and legs. I couldn't express myself. Fields went away, and I held my mother in my arms. But for many days to come I was as an actor in a drama, myself and another at once. Within, meanwhile, the reality was lurking.

Funeral of Nathaniel Hawthorne

IT RAINED continually the rest of the week in which my father died. The funeral was to be on Monday. People called to say the proper thing as they conceived it. Mrs. Emerson fantastically addressed me as "Young head of the house!"

I suggested that none of us should look at the dead face; and it was so agreed; we would keep the memory of him alive. But the three beloved ones decorated the coffin with flowers; and his friends, and all Concord, on the morning of the last day, passed beside the coffin in the church and looked down at the loved and honored mould of life that lay there. Then the long procession moved up the village street and round the Sleepy Hollow burying ground. The rain had ceased the night before, and the trees and grass sparkled with spring freshness, under the smile of the gentle sun. On the summit of the green hillock, under the tall pines, the grave was dug, and I stood on the brink, his widow and daughters beside me. They were serene: the drama still obsessed me, and I wished to show no more than a grave and suitable emotion.

We four were driven slowly back down the slope and to the gate of the enclosure. There, on each side of the way, stood men with gray heads and lowered eyes: my mother looked at them to right and left, surprised, and then said in a low voice, "Oh, to the widow!" giving herself for the first time that title, and accepting the homage for his sake. I felt that it touched her heart with a spiritual pleasure. Longfellow, Holmes, Emerson, Pierce, Whittier, Lowell, and the rest did reverence to her as she passed, for his sake, but also for her own. She was more known and loved than her selfless soul suspected. In moments like these, the truth shines forth, and we are fain to confess it.

A few days afterward, my mother received from Longfellow, the beautiful little poem:

> "How beautiful it was, that one bright day
> In the long week of rain!
> Though all its splendor could not chase away
> The omnipresent pain.
>
> .   .   .   .
>
> For the one face I looked for was not there,
> The one low voice was mute;
> Only an unseen presence filled the air,
> And baffled my pursuit.
>
> .   .   .   .
>
> Ah! who shall lift that wand of magic power,
> And the lost clue regain?
> The unfinished window in Aladdin's tower
> Unfinished must remain!"

We were thankful at this time for Franklin Pierce. When, six years before, my sister Una had been ill at Rome, and we thought she must die, Pierce was in Rome, and came often to our little flat on the Piazza Poli, near the Fountain of Trevi, whose mellow voice was audible in our rooms at night. Pierce had little to say; but he would stand or sit there among us, with an expression on his stern features that was like a rock of refuge in storm, and there flowed out from his presence waves of sympathy that gave us not so much hope as love and strength. He had always possessed this rare power of sympathy: thought for others rather than for himself.

When Pierce and his only son were on the train bound for Washington and his inauguration as President, there was a collision, and the boy, struck by a fragment of the wreck, was killed where he sat. The mother happened not to see the crushed body beside her, and Pierce had quickly taken off the voluminous cloak which men wore in those days, and flung it over the grievous spectacle. He passionately loved his wife, and when, not long after, she died, and Hawthorne came to the funeral, he and the sorrowing husband, standing beside the open grave while the coffin was being lowered into it, were exposed to a cold wind, and Pierce remembered that his friend was always sensitive to such exposure: he turned from the grave and turned up the collar of Hawthorne's overcoat.

In their youth, the two had been at Bowdoin together and became intimate friends. But Pierce had inherited a taste for strong liquor; he was powerful in body, strong-willed, and magnetic, so that he would occasionally lead his comrades into riotous scrapes. Hawthorne was no mollycoddle; but he was temperate, and by sheer force of character influenced Pierce to moderation.

Again, in after life, when Pierce had fulfilled his declared ambition to be President of the United States, Hawthorne drew from him a promise to abstain entirely from drink during his Presidency. And throughout those four arduous years, when political decisions of deep moment had to be made, Pierce held inviolably to this promise, in an era when drinking and drunkenness were a matter of course with politicians. No wonder then that the two men were friends!

Campus Events

SPEAKING of college popularity, I had been about to say that absence might be a cause of it; so the rustications—there were two or three of them in four years—would largely account for my classmates' partiality. Too much presence may wear out welcome. Meanwhile the Faculty had shifted their responsibility to the little clergyman; and the crew missed me in practice as well as in sentiment. By timing my withdrawals judiciously I could also enjoy the benefit of legend, which is as prone to flatter as to censure; and I myself, in addition to the free pleasures of country life, might attain an impartial view of the What and Why of mortal existence. College may impart culture—*"emollit mores, nec sinit esse feros"*—but a natural ferocity is not without its merits, and there can be too much emollient.

My old room, 3 Hollis, had an historic charm for me already. We had a hazing séance there once, the room crowded with a joyous throng of a dozen freshmen, as many sophomores, and a gallery of juniors to criticize the performance. Some one knocked down some one else, and there was a great skirmish—but just as things were about to become hectic, the door was opened, and there stood a member of the Faculty, by whom the poor victim of the fray was made the goat, as having been caught *flagrante*.

One day, I was returning from lunch with Will Morton, a crony, when he found a cow chewing her cud, looking out of his window. She had been admitted an hour before, and had acted as cows will, in or out of the proper place. Our efforts to get her out amused a group of sophomores, looking on, and proffering counsel. There was no recourse. Fortunately, Will's room was not carpeted with Aubusson or Persian rugs.

On the whole, the Med Fac, the famous hazing organization of the previous decade, had ceased to be formidable in my time. But an aggressive act against Jones and the college bell was brought off one rainy and gusty night, the doers (there was reason to think) being members of the freshman class. Hollis, and the building used for examinations, which carried the bell cupola on its ridgepole, cornered on each other, the gap between being some five feet, and the drop to the ground sixty. Imagine three desperadoes, at one o'clock of that rainy morning, crawling out of the attic dormer window of Hollis, making their way along the slippery slope of the roof to the corner, leaping thence to the slippery corner of the roof adjoining—darkness, wind, rain and death for a miss. Up the slope to the cupola, unship the bell, and overboard with it: then, return as you came. Desperadoes, truly!

Next morning, no clang of bell summoned the Harvard undergraduates to prayers, and Jones, the faithful toller of the bell, was defeated for once. Old Peabo intoned his prayer to vacant pews; but by nine o'clock the bell was going again, and we could be punctual for recitation. Jones, being interviewed, spoke solemnly. "If one of you boys had got killed, I'd have felt like resigning my post. Fun is all right, but getting killed is not fair play."

But this reminds me that at one in the morning I had arrived in Cambridge after a turnpike walk from Concord, starting at about ten Sunday night, and coming out between Hollis and Stoughton buildings into the college yard, I was nearly in collision with a heavy mass of something falling from above. It thumped down on the hard gravel walk, and lay moveless, seemingly dead; in the semidarkness I saw it was a man, and then that it was one I knew—a sophomore, Chamberlain. I suppose I shouted for help; in a few minutes a dozen fellows, more or less clad, surrounded the body.

With many bones broken, he groaned to be allowed to die—he had taken the leap from the top of the building in a suicide attempt; but he was patched up and set on his feet again. A year later, after watching a performer on the rings (on which he had himself been proficient), he shot himself in a hotel room. Was it from a broken heart or for broken bones? Rumor had it there was a woman concerned, when Chamberlain took that leap the year before. I have often thought about him, letting himself be restored to life, and then after a year, carrying out his purpose to die.

Then there was Braman, somewhat older than the rest of us freshmen, who defiantly wore a beaver—that is, top-hat, silk hat, dress hat, stovepipe—whatever may be its twentieth century name. He told us he was in constant peril from heart disease. The unwritten law forbade freshmen to wear beavers; every sophomore was marshaled against Braman, who declared that he would defend it to the death: "And let me tell you, fellows, death is what I mean: any physical struggle may cost me my life; but I'll die with my hat on!" There was the hat, to be knocked off with a mere flip of the wrist; but Joseph Balch Braman, with heart disease, was a cat that nobody dared bell.

Cupid Hodges
—Landon Longworth

AS UNIQUE as Braman, the Harvard freshman who wore his beaver in defiance of seventy-eight sophomores, and perhaps more attractive, was Cupid Hodges, as they called him, because he looked like the effigies of the god, or like the young Bacchus. The first I saw of him was his bare legs sticking up out of Flint Pond. I didn't know, at a distance, what they were; but Cupid was at home in the water and almost as much under as on it: he reared himself up as I drew near, and so our ac-

164

quaintance began, and lasted his lifetime. He was just under six feet, his face perfectly classic, his body all symmetry, power, and unconscious grace. He never attended a gymnasium, or knew an Indian club from a dumb-bell, but he had the strength and symmetry of the Immortals.

Cupid Hodges had a voice which, at its top compass, might have been audible across Boston Bay, without ceasing to be melodious; for he was born to music, and could have sung down the walls of Jericho. He finally went to Milan, where he bade fair to surpass all precedent; but the young giant took sick and died overnight.

One day he rowed up the Charles, a few miles beyond our boat-houses where his shell capsized; but instead of bothering to push it ashore, empty it and reëmbark, he climbed on top of it and floated down. He had nothing on but a pair of cotton knee-drawers, which soon slipped down to his knees, and then he kicked them off altogether. Thus he passed along between the educated Cambridge estates, singing wild songs, clothed in the *joie de vivre;* since the Lady of Shalott there had been nothing like it. He passed under Brighton Bridge, across which many market-women were going home. Cupid's songs, which were now of the Mississippi-boatman type, unsuited to virgin ears, had already attracted their attention from afar, and they lined the bridge-rail to see. They saw it all, and greeted it with cordial uproar, wavings, greetings, challenges, and whole-souled mirth: Cupid's repartee was more than adequate. Heralded thus, he came on down, in the golden afternoon, pagan-like a-sprawl, toward Camelot, ignoring our greetings, invitations and threats, and disappeared round the bend, still chanting. How he got home, we never learned.

But often, in the dead vast and middle of the night, we would be awakened by a mighty voice resounding under the stars—we knew it was Cupid!—and the stern professors would stir and mutter on their pallets, but Cupid sung on, incorrigible. He was a friend of mankind, male and female, but he was a son of the great god Pan, or Pan himself, and could not be subdued to our category.

Another memory is that of Landon Longworth: his nature and mind were in inverse proportion to his almost diminutive stature. As we trod the paths of the Green, the top of his head was hardly above my shoulder, but in mental feet and inches the discrepancy was rather the other way. He knew all the Law and the Prophets and rallied me on my ignorance. We were constantly together except when the curriculum divided us. What talks, expositions, impassioned arguments, scorn, jests, *anerithmon gelasma*—the mirth of the Olympians! I'm sure he wasn't older than I, and I think he was younger, speaking by the almanac; but not De Quincey nor Coleridge had read more books or could quote chapter and verse, at need, more punctually. His imagination was creative, and if the brooks of memory ran dry, he had at his command Amazons and Niles of invention.

William Hanlon's Fall from
the Flying Trapeze

AFTER Landon Longworth returned from his studies abroad, he went home to Cincinnati, and his death
happened soon after. Therefore I think of him as he
was in our earlier time.

We would take the horse-car to Boston three or four
times a week—there was straw on the floor, and the fare
was three cents—get a room at Parker's, have dinner.
Then awaited us the Negro Minstrels, or the Maffit
and Bartholomew performance, including a Pantomime,
and Annette La Pointe for the dancing. Nothing else
on two woman-legs could rival her charm. Impossible
to say just what it was, but even Isadora Duncan, in
after years, left me cold, comparatively speaking.

Occasionally our attention might be diverted to the
Howard Athenaeum, where the tremendous Helen
Western would be doing Mazeppa, bound, theoreti-
cally naked, on the bare back of a stallion shod with
fire. Round and round the track the steed docilely can-
tered, while Helen struggled with her cruel bonds. It
was only later that I discovered the historical fact that
Mazeppa was not a lady, and that he was rescued; but
I always felt something unreal in the performance, and

167

Landon was frankly sceptical, though even he had not read Byron's poem. But if the great stars shone, we would go to the Boston Theatre and palpitate to Charlotte Cushman, Ristori, Edwin Booth.

But it was not with Landon, but with General Pierce, that I went to see William Hanlon in his great act of Zampillaerostation. That bewildering title was written from end to end of the board-fences. The General liked acrobatic performances, and our seats were in the center of the dress circle so that William, in his stupendous leap, would alight on his little footstand close to us, thence to face about and take his more perilous plunge back again.

He made his bow before the audience, which filled the immense theater, poised himself on the stand, facing us, the trapeze in his right hand. As he stood he was calm and confident as a bird, and no deeper breath disturbed the silken luster on his chest.

The span of the gulf from the dress circle to the back of the stage looked impossible. Hanlon poised himself once more, the tiny trapeze grasped in both hands. Meanwhile, on the footstand at the back of the stage stood the assistant, whose difficult function it was to impel another trapeze which must meet Hanlon at a certain point in his leap, not an inch more or less. At the signal agreed upon, Hanlon leaped, and as he went, clewed himself up for a back somerset, on completing which he would grasp the approaching trapeze and swing back to the first stand at the back of the stage.

He did his part: but the assistant missed his cue by a fraction of a second or of an inch. Hanlon, traveling at

168

speed in mid-air, snatched at the return trapeze, missed it, and fell from a height of forty feet. His body struck the stage just beyond the footlights.

He struck flat on his back, and lay motionless. The spectators uttered a sort of hiss of consternation, General Pierce, starting to his feet, exclaimed, "The man is dead!" Two thousand persons in the great arena must have agreed with him. For the space of two breaths it seemed certain.

Then, the athlete stirred: he sat erect. We watched him, dumb with amazement. He got on his feet and stood for a moment; then he turned and began to walk steadily along the narrow gangway between the pit seats. He reached the vertical ladder and mounted it to the high stand close to the General and myself. There he caught the trapeze which the assistant tossed toward him, waited until the latter had taken his place, and, at the signal, leaped once again. This time he caught the coming bar, and the next moment stood safe aloft before us.

The applause was irregular, sporadic. The spectators were more stunned than the performer. One man near by muttered, "He did it on purpose!"—he was that sort of man. But though everybody knows that acrobats train to fall, if possible without breaking bones or meeting death, yet the most daring and skillful of them would not have risked the terrible hazard that Hanlon survived. But we also know that unless, after an accident, the performer immediately tries his act over again, he will never again muster courage for it. Hanlon therefore knew that he must choose, on the instant, between daring death and forsaking his career; he chose the former and beyond hope succeeded, in spite of the shock he had sustained. But the occasion was historic, and if any still live who, in their boyhood, witnessed it, they will have told the tale to their half-disbelieving great-grandchildren.

PART FOUR

Famous Friends
During Harvard Days

Oliver Wendell Holmes

THE BOYS—collegians—sat alphabetically; I was next to Ned Holmes, as long as he lived; youngest son of Oliver Wendell Holmes, handsome and lovable, and brilliant in scholarship; his famous brother had graduated some years before, and was now in the army, where he was badly wounded, and his father went south to search him out and bring him home; found him by chance on a train; and the pent-up emotions of the unexpected meeting were expressed in the New England words, "Hullo, Boy!"—"Hullo, Dad!" Fields, editor of the *Atlantic,* hastened to the Wayside to read the manuscript of the article Oliver Wendell Holmes wrote about it— one of his best. All our family were gathered to listen; Fields read admirably and we all laughed. Oliver Wendell, Jr., had survived, and is still at this writing,* high in place and honor,—but Edward died in his teens.

But let me take you back to a day in Harvard College, one hundred years ago. A young medical student glancing over a newspaper. Suddenly his face flushes, he starts to his feet—five feet five inches in his boots—and shouts out these words:

"Aye, tear her tattered ensign down" (and you know the rest).

* Justice Holmes died March 6, 1935.

For that newspaper had told him that the famous American frigate *Constitution,* which fought and defeated the British ships in the War of 1812, and was then lying in glorious retirement in the Navy Yard, scarred with the wounds of her battles—that famous veteran, for the sake of a few dollars upkeep to the country which she saved, was to be scrapped, and her sacred remains sold to junkmen for what they would bring! And the soul of that medical student was afire with patriotic indignation; and though but small of physical stature, his soul was tall enough to be seen from one end of our country to the other, and his words will be remembered and acclaimed for many generations.

"Old Ironsides"—as we lovingly called the famous ship—will be known and honored by our children's children: and it will be long, I think, before we forget the name of the young medical student, little as he himself expected fame from his apostrophe. But he was to live among us in love and honor for more than eighty-five years, followed by his likewise famous son, who on the Bench of the Supreme Court of the United States at an advanced age, and until 1932, added new honors to what had so long been honorable.

But it is of the father I am thinking now. He was a mainstay of American literature in prose and poetry, graceful, humorous, patriotic. His "Chambered Nautilus" had a great vogue; in pure humor, the "One-Hoss Shay" is immortal: and his renown in prose fiction rivals his verse. "The Autocrat of the Breakfast-Table" and its sequels, and the novels "Elsie Venner" and "The Guardian Angel," in spite of their Victorian flavor, are incomparable today.

He seems always to be writing on the spur of the moment. You would think he never could recapture that first, fine, careless rapture; but that is all in the day's work with Holmes: Wit and Holmes were one. But he was as quick to tears as to laughter, which was never ill-natured, nor tainted with vulgarity. All his prose and poetry were additional to his professional work in medicine, in which he was strenuous for nearly half a century. Meanwhile his meditations on mortal life made him a philosopher, and Darwinism could not unseat his religious faith.

In his mid-manhood he helped to found the *Atlantic Monthly Magazine* in which he resumed the "Autocrat" —which had been begun in some other defunct periodical of twenty years before—with the words, "As I was saying when I was interrupted." An interval of a generation could not abate the current of his vigorous thought. Those "Autocrat" essays took the stiffness out of American literature, and broke through all Victorian traditions. The pleasure he himself took in creating them is undisguised and adds to our own; he combines the wisdom of the sage with the candor of a boy. A home-loving boy, too: after his studies in professional schools in Europe, he never left New England, and seldom Cambridge and Boston, till his triumphal progress abroad in 1886, a few years before his death.

Holmes was never a recluse, but was out and abroad everywhere, in the familiar streets of his own city and the houses of his friends: it was he who named Boston the Hub of the Universe. He was the chief figure at club dinners and social assemblies, always with a poem to amuse and edify them. He was welcome as sunshine; as I intimated, his physical stature was far from com-

mensurate with his genius; but his figure was compact
and active as a bird, his step light and almost skipping,
as if he were too buoyant for plain walking; all this adds
to his charm—if brevity be the soul of wit, Holmes was
wit's embodiment. He seemed superior to the tedium of
earth and to have found the elixir of the old magicians.
He was our beloved Genius of Good Cheer.

Last Impressions of Holmes
—James Mills Peirce

MEETING Oliver Wendell Holmes, Sr., in his walks,
one could feel in advance the radiation of his pleasure;
as his friend Emerson would put it, his face "mantled
with mirth." But it was no conventional grimace; he
had a joyful question to put, or a happy thing to say,
to leave you the better for the meeting; it was his instinct to be sociable. He loved physical existence, and
would make others love it. He was like a child, but not
with childish thoughtlessness. In his professional studies, and in his metaphysical speculations, his mind continually questioned the Mysteries of Life: like Milton's
Angels in "Paradise Lost," he meditated on "Fate, Freewill, Foreknowledge absolute" and, not content with
the answers of others to the Great Riddles, must seek his
own. The make and movement of his thought were not
conventional, but original; in the old Puritan times he
would have been a dissenter.

But the simile of a bird recurs in thinking of him—

not so much the Bird of Paradise as the cheerful Robin Redbreast; chirping, twittering, singing, and hopping about. On the spur of the moment he would chirp an epigram to be remembered for generations. Yet he never strove to take the lead; though genial as Robin Goodfellow, he was modest as a girl. Yet he cared for conventional reticences, but confessed his joys and griefs. Holmes opened his heart for all to be glad or sorry with him.

Not long before his death, I went to see him at his new house in lower Beacon Street, Boston. The house was sumptuous in size and furnishings—almost incongruous with the beloved little man who sat solitary in the great room opening on the Back Bay. He was busy with manuscripts, and explained he was preparing them for the publisher of his last book—"One Hundred Days in Europe." His face was crisscrossed with little wrinkles, and the former effervescence would subside at times, as with good wine that has stood too long. He would gaze off into the great empty rooms, as if seeking the wife who had gone, and the beloved friends, Longfellow, Lowell, Hawthorne, Fields: only echoes and specters remained. The passion and activity of the "Old Ironsides" period was gone, and the Famous Autocrat must lie henceforth at his moorings, awaiting the Unknown End.

I recall the noble moral of that other poem of his—"The Chambered Nautilus" which he had lived to vindicate:

> Build thee more stately mansions, O my soul,
> As the swift seasons roll!
> Leave thy low-vaulted past!
> Let each new temple, nobler than the last,

Shut thee from Heaven with a dome more vast,
Till thou at length art free,
Leaving thine outgrown shell by life's unresting sea.

And so, speaking of young Edward Holmes, who sat beside me in my freshman class in Harvard, brought about this digression on his worthy and illustrious father—the temptation was too great to be withstood. But back once more in our classroom. Here happened my adventure with Professor James Mills Peirce which may as well be told here.

He was a profound mathematician: he spoke with deliberation and distinctness, as if enunciating a problem in the higher mathematics, and wore an air of inviolable authority, placid because unassailable. Such was Peirce's frigid front.

Naturally, when the professor and I came into contact, I foresaw my finish. He would sweetly hand me a cup of poison in the guise of a problem; I would take it to the blackboard and write down the terms; stand dully staring at it for a few minutes, then rub it out and return to my place. Peirce, inscrutable, would make no comment; only, one day, he said, "Hawthorne, are you never going to make me a recitation?"

I answered with the quietness of desperation:

"Professor, I really study your book more than any other. But I don't understand what it says. And when you call me up, I forget all I know. I'm sorry—but that's all!"

After hours, he asked me to call at his room in Holworthy, at eight that evening. What novel form of execution was the old Torquemada thinking up for me?

At eight sharp I knocked at his door, and he opened it himself. He smilingly shook hands, giving me a powerful grip, and pointed to two easy-chairs facing the cheerful coal fire.

"Sit down: it is a pleasure to see you; make yourself comfortable: I have been considering your case; it is interesting. But first, may I ask, do you drink?"

I was taken aback, but my conscience was pretty clear: my last drink, and first, had been in the room of the silken laps and the snowdrift plunge at Lexington. I answered, "I had some whiskey a year ago . . ."

"And do you prefer rye or bourbon?"

As he spoke he opened a corner closet, and brought out two bottles which he set on the table: I pointed, at hazard, to one of them. "Bourbon! You and I have the same taste!" He seemed gratified. The upshot of this amazing drama was that he told me he would no longer call on me for recitations, but wished me to continue to attend, and to study the problems, and at the end of the term he would give me the average mark.

"Do you agree?" he asked holding out his hand.

An angel, masked as Mephistopheles! I returned his grip with all my heart, and we kept the faith forever.

A German Project—
Illumination

WITH the end of my Harvard adventure in sight, the chemistry of events began to boil together in its cauldron things seemingly unrelated until, out of the mixture, suddenly appeared the apparition of Europe, and more particularly of Germany, and still more definitely of the old city of Dresden, in Saxony, on the river Elbe; with its Green Vaults full of treasures of antiquity; its great gallery of paintings, including Raphael's divine Madonna and Child; its opera house, where Wagner and all his mighty forerunners had their home: its nearness to Leipsic, where the toys were made; and its incomparable beer, foaming in hundreds of hospitable kellers and breweries. Also, and decisively, there was a Realschule there, famous as the best in the world for training civil engineers—and I had decided to make civil engineering my profession. The preliminary step was to learn how to read, write, and speak the German language; but that would be child's play. While that was proceeding, we could be making up our minds what to do with the Wayside. And before that even, I might be taking a course at the Lawrence Scientific School, across the yard from the Harvard buildings, in order to get some notion of what civil engineering was. That would take up a year; so there was plenty of time for other preparations.

Hitherto, my predilections had been for rowing, walking, and art. Of the former activities, *"Sat prata biberunt,"* as Virgil remarks in one of his Eclogues. The latter propensity was derived from my mother, to whom art in all its forms was native, and who during our long sojourn in Europe had lovingly absorbed the achievements of the Masters. She was also gifted as a teacher, and encouraged my sketch-book industries in England and on the Continent; and during the last weeks of our stay abroad she brought home one evening a wonderful little volume—the Book of Ruth transcribed from the Bible in old English black-letter, with borders faithfully reproduced from missals painted in the fourteenth century by Giulio Clevio in his monastic cell; with little miniatures, too, of figures and scenes in the story, thanks to Owen Meredith and Noel Humphreys.

There had been a revival of the art of illumination, and this little book is the crown of the study. Nothing to rival it was afterward produced; but manuals of practical instruction were published; and the illuminated Bibles and missals of the Middle Ages were shown in public museums and libraries; over which I pored at opportunity; and thereupon attempted the fascinating industry on my own account. Some of my efforts were entrusted to book shops for exhibition, at the dignified price of one hundred dollars each. Several of them were bought, and they may turn up centuries hence at auctions of bibelots, for the paints were the best of Windsor and Newtons, and the gold was pure from the mine. I spared no expense, actually using my $100 checks for the purpose—an unusual dissipation, for a husky lad in his teens. It had its useful side; for afterward, when I came to make mechanical designs in General McClellan's New York office, I had the technique at my fingers' ends.

So much, then, for art. The German project was brought to a head by Miss Mary Vandevoort, who visited us at a favorable moment. She had dwelt several years in Dresden. She was charmingly frank, yet a mystery, as maiden ladies of sixty are, I suppose, apt to be. Later, in Dresden, on one of my frequent visits to her little flat, she asked me to fetch her cloak from the clothes-closet; while searching there, I came upon a pair of man's trousers. What could they mean in a maiden lady's closet? She chuckled in her amused way: "They're a pair of brother Jim's that he left here; they make me feel more comfortable." In short, she was simple, cultivated, humorous and delightful, and she had secrets which she liked to think about, and never reveal. So it was due to her that we arrived in Dresden a year later.

My experience at the Lawrence Scientific School didn't minister to my self-esteem, or increase my fondness for mathematics, but I had the fortune to get in touch with James Russell Lowell. My mother wrote to ask him if he would give me a little preliminary insight into German; Lowell cordially undertook, for Hawthorne reasons, the mollifying of my barbarism. My mother used to say of him, "He glares, from the red jungle of his beard," and all I had known of him up to then, had been that glare as he walked Cambridge streets. And of his daughter Mable, nothing. I couldn't think of her, when I got to know her, as of anything other than a religious recluse, a sort of nun, vowed to no less a bridegroom than Christ. So I got a shock when her betrothal to a young farmer was announced. I would as little have expected Miranda to marry Caliban. But he prospered greatly in his making of a famous brand of sausages, and I am sure he was the best of good fellows.

James Russell Lowell

JAMES RUSSELL LOWELL, as you have seen, was a delightful companion, even to a boy so unrepentantly ignorant as I was when I came to know him personally, in 1866–68. He had not then begun his diplomatic career. Apart from his writings and his diplomatic avocations, he was an interesting personage, solitary, but resolved to be a poet, and from his thirty-first year onward he wrote and published poetry. But he was really of a sociable nature, and like many patricians, democratic in theory. It is easier to condescend than reach up, and young Lowell, when at a loss for fitting companions of his own social rank, would put on a rough suit of clothes, take tobacco and a pipe, and ramble forth in quest of Yankee farmers and such like: would sit beside them on a log and engage them in talk, getting insight into their native qualities, and remembering their phrases, idioms, and pronunciation for future use in his own literature—as the famous series of "Biglow Papers" bears witness. I don't know that a better "dialect" was ever written; indeed these Papers surpass the dialect itself, and one might almost suspect him of inventing it, as Bret Harte is charged with inventing his wild-West speech and his stories. But it conveys the accepted character of the speakers and their point of view, and outdoes them in wit and humor, not to speak of satire.

Satirist, wit, and humorist Lowell certainly was, and he made them tell, in politics as well as elsewhere. John Bull could make no adequate rejoinder to his criticisms, and it is to the credit of John's magnanimity that he welcomed him as Minister to the Court of St. James's a dozen years after Hosea Biglow had ceased to call attention to British hoggishness. We have never sent a representative to that country who was better liked there, or more congenial than he—though he never apologized for his squibs, or abated his Yankee independence. In truth he was more English at bottom than the English themselves, and could write his well-known essay "on a certain condescension of foreigners" because he himself was such a master of condescension. He knew English literature from top to bottom, and could talk Chaucer like a gentleman of the thirteenth century.

He was one of the family, and criticized so keenly because members of the same family commonly are inspired and equipped for that sort of intimate animadversion; they know where to hit. Meanwhile the breadth of his sympathies is indicated by his contemporaneous flights of sentiment and imagination: we have all been familiar with his lively query, "What is so rare as a day in June?" and some are still living who have taken off their hats at the grave music of his "Commemoration Ode." It may be admitted, however, that editors of current magazines would be readier to open their pages to such an effusion as "The Courtin'"—a bit of homely realism.

The fact that Lowell's literary proclivities carried him in directions so diverse may lend weight to the suspicion that he never was nor could be an honest-togoodness divine-afflatus poet. He knew too much, was too scholarly, never wholeheartedly believed in his own poetic faculty. He was a victim of too early culture and education; his aristocratic environment sapped the integrity of his faith. If a man's memory is not a virgin page for his own perceptions, but is written and crossed over with the thoughts of former persons, he is in constant doubt as to whether it is "original," or merely giving a fresh wording to old stuff; whereas, if he writes from the heart, he is free from anxiety, for one man's heart can never see or feel like any other's. A true poet, if he has brains, can make occasional use of them; the lyrics of Keats and Shelley, and the songs of Shakespeare, carry no taint of brains, but are fresh as morning skies and flowers.

There are happy moments when Lowell almost forgets himself as an American gentleman of the highest type and most refined culture and as a scholar of wide erudition. It was a great deal to forget, but he managed it, now and again. He had brains, pressed down and running over, and they were graceful sirens to mislead him. He himself was aware of it, but, unlike Ulysses, he hadn't taken the precaution to have himself bound to the mast before venturing near the siren's isle.

He was more satisfactory in prose, because not aiming so high; his essays are charming reading. One book of his—"Fireside Travels"—which I found on that bookshelf of my father's was a delight and an education to me.

Lowell had visited Europe for a couple of years, previous to taking the chair of belles-lettres at Harvard in succession to Longfellow: that was in 1855; from 1857 to 1858 he edited the *Atlantic Monthly,* and afterward the *North American Review*. Then the government appointed him minister to Spain, and afterward to England. So his long and honorable services to literature and learning had their reward; he had realized whatever success and happiness were possible for such a man. I had renewed my contact with him during his official residence in London, and witnessed his complete conquest of the British: he was enchanting as after-dinner speaker; his aspect, his voice, his wit, point, and skill, his warm friendliness, made him incomparable.

When James Russell Lowell undertook my initiation into the German language, I sat with him in his study two or three evenings a week. The study was a big room on the left of the doorway as you enter the house, and in every way delectable. I have always purred in libraries and have been caressed by some of the best. The soft glow of bindings along the shelves, the atmosphere of meditative leisure, the happy pilgrimages through the alcoves which imagination promises—the more alluring because never to be realized; the actual opening of here and there a volume, like a door ajar where Beauty is disrobing, the intent perusal of here and there a page, as if Rhodopis had relented for a breathing-space—I can't remember when I wasn't subject to such emotion in the magic atmosphere of books. And though I couldn't indulge my wandering proclivity in Lowell's library, I was brought in touch with the spirit of Faust —whose history, as Goethe dreamed it, was chosen to be the theme of our studies during that winter.

It was, in the circumstances, a singular choice; but I was the sole pupil Lowell had ever attempted, and he was not a man for grammars and dictionaries. So he took me at once to the headwaters, and I approved of the plan, though, to tell the truth, at the end of our collaboration I knew little of the German language, conversationally speaking, and he, recognizing my un-ploughed and unsowed condition, gracefully adopted the only course practicable: he would assign me a passage from the poem, courteously assume at our next meeting that I had mastered it, and would then proceed to read-out and construe it himself, giving me the benefit both of the great poet's visual, and of his own eloquent, comprehension of it; I have never enjoyed German so much since, though I was to pass refreshing hours with Heinrich Heine's lyrics and his prose "Reisebilder"; and with some of Jean Paul's incomparable Ixion-flights.

I like to recall those hours I was privileged to spend alone with Lowell before the log fire in his library at Elmwood. I can hardly imagine that my mother expected me to acquire any practical familiarity with German from those interviews; and as a fact what I did learn was Lowell himself—as much of him as a boy could comprehend; he gave me generously whatever he thought I could assimilate. Ostensibly, we read Goethe's "Faust" together—in reality he read and I listened.

A Journey with Franklin Pierce

DIVERGENCE in views of statesmanship could not affect the bond of friendship that existed between Franklin Pierce and Nathaniel Hawthorne; and the lat-

187

ter, much against his taste, wrote the cogent little campaign biography of Pierce which aided no little in his election. And almost his last gesture in this world was to dedicate his book "Our Old Home" to his friend, with a preface, which his publishers vainly besought him not to publish, lest it destroy the sale of the book— so keen were political animosities and prejudices then. In the preface he defined exactly his attitude and his reasons; the pusillanimity of disguising truth for the sake of copyrights was not in his code of ethics. That the seven-year sojourn in Europe had been due to Pierce, was but a side-issue. He loved and respected the man, and no other time appeared to him so suitable for declaring it as when the currents of public favor ran against him.

My mother had a cordial affection for Pierce, and he valued it for her sake as well as for Hawthorne's. She confided in him as in a brother, and when, in the summer after my father's death, he proposed taking me on a trip through the northern states, she gladly consented. He was fond of driving, and had a pair of blooded black horses, whose regular pace was twenty miles an hour (though he would seldom call on them for that), and they seemed fresh at the end of a long day's journey. Of course autocars were unimagined in 1864, and horse travel is more interesting and enjoyable.

Once, driving through picturesque New England, as we approached a fine old dwelling, withdrawn from the highway, Pierce said, with a smile, "This is one of my bitterest enemies in the Presidential campaign." We drove up to the door, and an old farmer came out in pants and suspenders and, when he recognized his visitor, gave him a grim look. His sons followed their father with sullen brows. Pierce got down from his seat and stepped up to them, hands outstretched, the great gentleman who had worn his country's honors, democratic, simple, friendly. "Old foes make good friends when the fight is over! Buchanan and I have shaken hands—so must you and I." In a few minutes they were all (as the old-fashioned phrase was) hanging on his accents. The old man grinned and melted; the boys were fascinated. None of them would ever forget that ten minutes under the shade of the butternut trees. Pierce seemed pleased as he drove away. "You see, Julian," he remarked, "men are swayed less by political theories than by man-to-man!" And I digested, as best I might, my first lesson in politics or statesmanship. Men high in public life must be actors.

The route we followed bent to the right, and after a day or two we were approaching the seacoast. We halted at Rye Beach, now, I believe, a fashionable resort, then almost unknown, but Pierce had put up a little cottage there. From Great Boar's Head, a promontory on the south, Pierce pointed out a lighthouse on a ridge of rocks, about fifteen miles out, not unknown in earlier New England annals.

"Your father and I spent a week out yonder," he said; "an old political ally of mine lives there—Captain Laighton. We'll hire a boat tomorrow and make a call on him. I believe they are putting up a hotel."

Pierce and I took a swim to rid ourselves of the dust of travel. Bathing suits were unknown in that remoteness. "You're well set up for a lad of seventeen," Pierce remarked, glancing me over. "Your father was a strong man, and very active—could jump, standing, as high as his chin, and walk all day. I was heavier than he, but I think he could have outfought me. Longfellow was a slim, peaceable little chap, handsome, but your father was the finest-looking man I ever saw."

Pierce had been in law and politics, but when we had our quarrel with Mexico, he went with General Taylor and fought through the war: it was then that they made him Brigadier General. We had always addressed Pierce as General—he didn't like his other title. I had already heard the outline of his Mexican career, and that his rise in rank had been due to bravery and capacity shown in action. He had been wounded, and the scar was visible in front of his right shoulder. His chest was impressive, and the great muscles of his arms and legs; his bearing was always erect and soldierly, and his coats buttoned up to the throat in military fashion. But he had never finally discontinued drink. He was taken seriously ill two years after, and I went up to his New Hampshire home to see him. Little more than the massive skeleton of the man seemed left, as he lay in bed. Yet some months later I saw him pass, as I was sitting in the window of the Boston Athenaeum. He was talking to a man with forceful gestures and walking with the step of a commander. He died, however, before seventy.

After our swim at Rye Beach, Franklin Pierce and I boarded a little smack and were put across to Appledore Island, where we were met by the heroic figure of Cedric Laighton, smiling a welcome through his vast yellow beard and in his laughing blue eyes—he was the younger son. His black-haired and bearded brother Oscar ran the new three-story hotel, which was three hundred feet long and had a cupola on top with a wide veranda all along the front; it stood facing the west, along the summit of the great rock which was Appledore. But none of these persons interested me as much as did the young lady who now came forward from a rock-ledge. Our meeting was a glorious miracle, like the meetings of lovers in the Arabian Nights.

General Pierce observed us; and after I had been with him to be presented to the old Viking father of the two stalwart sons, he said, "Julian, you seem to have fallen on your feet here; I shall have a few days' business in Boston: would you like to stay at the hotel for a week?" A graceful and noble gesture, I thought it. He took the smack back to the mainland, and the Golden Girl and I wandered off over the rocks and far away. I will say of her that she was a cousin of Lily Nelson, and that we had met once before, not long after my father's funeral. We now felt that a loving and lovers' Providence had us in charge and that Appledore was Eden.

But this is a sober quasi-autobiography, not a fiction romance or love story; and there is still much to relate about Concord and Harvard which has little to do with the Golden Girl. In the intervals of that seven-day Eternity I smoked a pipe with the old Viking, and made close friends with his Viking sons, not without a premonition of summers to come.

During our sea-and-land journey from Appledore Island to Concord, General Pierce asked me how I liked college. I replied that I liked the fellows (meaning my classmates) very well, that I enjoyed the gymnasium, and told him the fact that I had a larger chest-measure than any of the others, and that I didn't much mind the studies, except mathematics. I added that I had rowed

Number Three in our class crew, and even had a chance of getting into "The Harvard" Crew. My particular friends in the class were Landon Longworth and Charley Gage, though of course the others were all right. Mr. Gurney, I said, was my great friend among the professors (he taught Latin, you will recall). But "now, of course," I remarked gravely, "I must give up Harvard and go to work to earn my living and support the family."

The General listened attentively, but made no immediate rejoinder. Finally he asked, "Have you chosen your profession?"

No, I hadn't thought about that. I should like to be an explorer in Africa, like Livingstone, and a naturalist, like Mr. Agassiz or Mr. Thoreau. I liked to live outdoors, and sleep in a tent, or in the open air. I would think it over during the rest of the vacation.

"Have you talked with Mr. Hillard about this?" When I shook my head, he went on: "Hillard was a friend of your father, a scholar and a good lawyer and a critic of literature and art. Your mother is fond of him and trusts him: he has charge of your family property. In a talk with him after your father's death, I got the impression that both your parents were looking forward to your finishing your time at college, and that funds were available assuming that your habits were not extravagant."

He went on to tell me that Longfellow had written verses in his boyhood and was studious; but that my father had not decided what he would do; that my forefathers had owned ships in the East India trade and sailed them, or had farms, and that they had been well off. The first emigrant fought the Indians, and showed

talent as a statesman: and an important letter, written
to King George at the time, taking an independent
stand, was attributed to the first Hawthorne emigrant.
Some later Hawthornes were judges.

"I remember your father mentioned one of them as
having incurred a curse from one of the witches; he
ascribed the subsequent decay of the fortunes of the
family to that—but not quite seriously, I think," the
General remarked.

As we drove slowly along towards Boston, behind his
beautiful horses General Pierce continued to tell me
more of my ancestors and my father as he had known
him, saying, "You already know all this probably: but
I like to speak of your father, who was my dearest and
most honored friend." And thus he told me that my
father was a brilliant boy, but not inclined to schooling:
that he dominated boys of his own age, and that he
might have gone to sea, but an accident to his foot
obliged him to stay indoors for a year or two, during
which he did a great deal of reading in all sorts of
books; that my grandmother Hawthorne's brother, then
his uncle Robert Manning, who had money, persuaded
him to go to Bowdoin, where he and Pierce met.

During that never-to-be-forgotten ride Franklin Pierce
told me that a classmate of my father's, Horatio Bridge,
persuaded him that he was a born writer; perhaps his
habit of reading inclined him in the same direction, and
after graduation, he shut himself up in his room and
lived as a hermit for the next ten or a dozen years; he
burned most of what he wrote, and signed what he
published in the periodicals of the day with fictitious
names—he didn't wish to be known as an author, unless

as a successful one. He received small pay, often none at all; he lived and had his meals in the house on Union Street in Salem, built by my great-grandfather, not wishing to draw upon the small property left to his mother, nor to accept aid from his uncle Robert Manning.

He asked me if I had thought of becoming a writer. I replied that my father had advised me not to.

"It is natural for a boy with your vigorous frame to want an outdoor life: but neither is that remunerative; and even great naturalists like Agassiz and Livingstone and Thoreau are not rich men. Besides you would be separated from your mother and sisters." He went on to suggest civil engineering; but a successful engineer must be a mathematician, and that was my weakest point.

I now began to feel uneasy; how could I join Livingstone in Africa, leaving my mother and sisters unprotected in Concord? And there were other matters.

As if he had divined my thoughts the General observed, "Some day, too, you might think of marriage." And I remembered that he had seen the meeting of the Golden Girl and myself at the island. Nevertheless, this was the first time that the thought of marriage, with its attendant conditions, had occurred to me; the very power of love itself had dazzled out of sight the conventional consequence. Marriage!—and to support a wife, together with my own family!—and I a boy of seventeen and still a freshman! I was suddenly bewildered and dumb-stricken.

The wise General gave me time to recover, and we drove along under the maples, whose golden leaves were beginning to fall. He advised me not to hurry my decision, to talk with Hillard, and get the benefit of his counsel. A decision which is to affect one's whole life should be well considered. "I suppose," he said, "it is to avoid hurry that the four years of college are given."

So this great gentleman, who had sat in the high seat of government, was interested, for the sake of the life-long friendship with my father, in my boyish affairs. I don't suppose I fully appreciated it then; I was used to having people like me, and finding life pleasant. I haven't attempted, at this distance of years, to quote the General verbatim, but what he said went deep into me, and I have never forgotten the substance of it. In Boston, we called on Mr. Fields, and I afterward went to Mr. Hillard's office; and with all this accumulated wisdom, I went home to the Wayside, and meditated, perhaps, on the Golden Girl of Appledore.

The upshot of it all was that I was to resume my college life, and to postpone meanwhile my grandiose project of being the Head of the Family and responsible for it. My short effort at being mature was over, and I was glad of it, for, whatever the Faculty might want or expect of me, there was no doubt about my being welcome to the class crew. My inclinations were more social and athletic than studious, and during the sixty years since then, I have never regretted it. But no doubt, college in the 1860's was very different from what it has grown to be today.

The consumptive young English university graduate who came out to New England in 1637, and died after preaching there for a year or so, left three to four thousand dollars to start a college in the precarious wilderness. Others contributed, and named the college Harvard, after him.

Religion and education were sisters in those times. Two hundred years later, when I arrived, this sisterhood had not altogether been disallowed. Most of the undergraduates had had religious influences at home, were sons of "gentlemen," and were not looking forward to using college training to facilitate making a living, but to acquire polite culture for society; often wouldn't expect to make a living at all, but to subsist on the inherited family income, or become lawyers and statesmen like General Pierce, or doctors like Oliver Wendell Holmes, or poets like Longfellow, or story writers like my father, or even, if needs must, professors in a university. But sons of gentlemen were expected to live as gentlemen, or to starve as gentlemen if it came to that, but never to become hucksters—to drop below their proper station. American Democracy, in short, was aristocratic at bottom.

PART FIVE

Family Happenings—
Comments on the Writings
of Nathaniel Hawthorne

The Author Gets Acquainted
with Literature

ON THE top shelf of my father's library were ranged a score or more of little paper-bound volumes, yellow and dog-eared and worn, printed in very small type, and in the French language, with which I was not too familiar. They had evidently been pretty thoroughly read in some long-past time: I picked out a page or two here and there, but didn't happen upon anything intriguing: and Voltaire seemed to have been prolix to an intimidating degree. I had heard that he had been famous, but I decided that my time to master those numerous little books had not yet arrived.

I was eighteen at the time, and in Harvard. But I know now that boys ought not to enter college before the age of forty—they are not ripe for it before then. The four years, between seventeen and twenty-one, are not misspent, however, in an environment like Harvard, Yale, Oxford, or Cambridge; the companionship of the other undergraduates is beneficial, and to be apprised of the existence of the several branches of learning and culture, though the college Faculty undoubtedly exaggerate the present importance of such matters. Just a glance over the general lay of the land is enough, and the youth also measures himself against his fellows, and finds out what his comparative stature in his future life in the world will be. Meanwhile, if he be of a wholesome nature, he will develop himself physically, and thereby ensure himself a sound heart and good lungs up to fourscore and beyond.

But as I was saying, I abandoned the Voltaire shelf in my father's library, and ranged lower. About midway down, I came upon an unobtrusive quartet of books very dilapidated, the green board covers defaced. I opened one of them: "The Adventures of Peregrine Pickle," by Tobias Smollett. "Peregrine" indicated that the hero was a traveler; "Pickle," that he was apt to get into scrapes. Running over the pages, I saw that his adventures had been various and amusing. At this time, I had not become acquainted with "Pickwick": this story seemed to belong to an older generation; it was not too long: it promised well. I lapsed into the big easy-chair, that idle Saturday afternoon, and began my companionship with the great Georgian novelist. "Peregrine" was not illustrated: Hogarth or Cruikshank might have done it; but in fact it was well enough without them. The text painted better pictures than any artist could design. Here was something not unworthy to stand in the same row with the mighty Cervantes.

Old English humor unafraid! What a delightful discovery for a boy of eighteen! The living persons whom I knew—Emerson, Thoreau, Bill Simmons, and the rest—appeared pale and inexpressive beside these hearty and forthright people. The warm color of intense human life flowed into my nostrils. With what simplicity and point the whole thing was portrayed, so that the book with its printed pages disappeared, and I was present in person at every scene: Peregrine and I were in one pickle after another; we throbbed together in suspense, we triumphed in unlooked-for rescues and victories. What a genial, natural, comical, moving race of happenings; what artless disclosures of the currents and undercurrents of human existence! Here at last was the cordial reality of things. The date of the story was the eighteenth century. People lived then. Had anyone ventured to be alive since then?

I was to hear of Thackeray's lament, in after years, that no novel since "Tom Jones" had dared to paint a man at full length and as he was. I found "Tom Jones" on the same shelf with "Peregrine": it was very good, and it had a most artful plot, which took some of the reality out of the whole performance; I didn't at the time know the name "picaresque," but my ignorance didn't prevent me from feeling that it was the true, right form of fiction. Let there be no beginning, middle, or end—take a chunk out of life and set it down to tell itself. I settled myself deeper in my easy-chair and wished I could read the book more slowly, or that the last page would keep at a distance forever. But it raced toward me; and I was comforted only by observing that there was another book by the same author on the shelf.

Yes, the world, not college, teaches you what you need just when you need it, and the lesson sticks. College teaches good manners and redeems from vulgarity. And if the liberal arts are less insisted upon now than then, more's the pity. Learning how to make a living is a poor substitute. It is painful to see a young fellow who knows too much—or a coed either.

Your brains, children, are the least valuable and individual parts of you. They are poor, promiscuous servants on the road of Life.

Maria Mitchell

WE HAD left England, after four years' life there, and were on our way to Rome, by way of France, when we were joined by Maria Mitchell, who had been a companion of our governess Ada Shepard at an Ohio college.

Now Maria Mitchell was a plain, New England old maid, from Gloucester, Massachusetts, but she was the greatest woman astronomer of her time; and, though she died long ago, her time can't be said to have ended yet. My infantine affections were lavished upon her, not without return. These relations continued between us for more than fifty years; the last time I saw her in the flesh was during the late eighties, when she was professor of astronomy at Vassar College; she was and looked just the same as a generation before—rather handsomer, I thought, with her gray hair, brilliant eyes, and good-humored dignity. She could have led an army or ruled a nation, but she was a woman to the core, with the lovely foibles of her sex.

It was her first trip abroad, and she was as fresh to the world as she was wise in learning; and her fine, aromatic New England quality affected us like a breath of the pine-woods and sea spray; but it was her family relation (so to say) with the stars that fascinated me, and I besieged her with questions. After a day or two, she was "Aunt Maria" for all time to come.

The steamer that took us to Civita Vecchia, the port for Rome, was the size of a large tugboat; the weather was perfect; at night the skies were clear and the constellations deployed before our astronomer as before a recognized field marshal. Aunt Maria and I established ourselves in a favorable position near the stern, and there she told me the names of the constellations and of the planets. Having been told that those three nice stars close together were called Orion's Belt, I at once informed my father that they were O'Brien's Belt, and so they were to the entire family ever after, but not until some laughter had been heard.

We got to Civita Vecchia toward evening, and must ride up to Rome, several hours' journey, in a stage-coach with four horses; the way was much infested by brigands: a party had been held up and robbed two days before. The coach was an old rattletrap, but spacious, and our party of seven, including Ada Shepard and Aunt Maria, managed to squeeze into it. Not to scare us children, the brigands were referred to by our elders as a sort of joke; and to carry it out, my father poured several handfuls of gold scudi into an umbrella, which he put into the straps in the roof of the vehicle, provided for such purposes. Aunt Maria put her fortune into her stocking. "Nobody'll search me," she declared valiantly.

At the last moment we learned that the government mail-coach was to follow close behind us, and the men on it were armed. That relieved the tension, and although twice or thrice, as we rumbled along in the dusk, between the high banks of the road, we saw men with wide-brimmed hats, knee breeches, and long guns in their hands looking down at us, they didn't open fire; the lights of the mail-coach were close behind us; and Aunt Maria held my hand tight all the time. But we didn't converse about the constellations; and, though Ada made occasional attempts to inform us as to the historic associations of the road, she too was pale and preoccupied; and there were murmurs of relief, when, at last, by flaring gas jets, we pulled up at the Porto del Popolo, and the gold was retrieved from the umbrella (Aunt Maria let hers stay where it was); and the customs officers made motions as if to search her baggage, but forbore when my father produced a scudo or two with an air of good-fellowship.

In another moment we were actually in Rome, bumping over cobblestone pavements, and passing below a very tall, pointed thing which Ada, now her cheerful self again, told us was an Egyptian obelisk. It was winter, and very cold, and the obelisk evidently hadn't brought the Egyptian climate along with it.

Aunt Maria took an apartment—a *piano*—in an old immense house in the Via Bocca di Leone; but she met us for explorations nearly every day. She and Ada and I usually found ourselves together; churches, picture galleries, the Vatican, St. Peter's; the Coliseum, the Forum—those two women were unweariable, though they were terribly tired by dinner time, but were up and at it again next morning early. They talked to each other about the beauties and wonders, and I listened, but understood little, though I loved Aunt Maria more and more. And whenever, since then, I think of Rome, I see it partly through her eyes, and hear echoes of her naïve comments, full of New England common sense and honest admiration. To be in Rome was the realization of a dream of a lifetime, and she was perfectly happy. Then, after the boy had grown up into something else, I went to Vassar to lecture there on "The Art of Fiction." Many faces met me on my arrival, but withdrawn a little to the rear, looking on, was a face which made the others dim to me; my own Aunt Maria, just the same as in Rome, but dearer than ever.

A Hawthorne Ghost Story

MY MOTHER had always felt a kind of sympathy with that kind of spiritual speculation which we call occultism, not in its grosser phases, but as a deeper insight into the realm of causes, and, as often happens to persons so inclined, several instances occurred in her experience which seemed to give substance to her persuasion—messages seemingly from another world, unaccountable presences, and the like.

Living with us then was Miss Ada Shepard, our governess. Much against her own liking she was endowed with mediumistic powers—to the extent, at least, that if she took a pencil in hand and put herself into a receptive or neutral mood she would presently begin to write sentences which purported to be messages from disembodied spirits. When Mrs. Browning mentioned her interest in spiritualism to my mother, she innocently disclosed to the English poetess Miss Shepard's unusual powers.

Mrs. Browning at once besought Miss Shepard to

give us an example of her mediumistic writings, to which poor Ada, much against her wish, finally acceded. The session began, and was followed at intervals by several others, much to the delight of Mrs. Browning, though her husband vowed himself a skeptic from the start. The result brought to light what might be termed a sort of Hawthorne ghost story: the "messages," which at first were very pious and heavenly, gradually became sinister and unpleasant, as if from a lower order of spirits, and the séances were discontinued; we moved from Florence to Rome and the matter was quite forgotten.

After a couple of years, we returned to New England, and it was not until after my father's death, in 1864, that I, browsing in his library, came across a folio volume of Sir Philip Sidney's "Arcadia" in which was found the signature of Daniel Hawthorne, who had commanded the brig *Fair America* in the War of the Revolution.

The printed text of this dilapidated little volume interested me less than did the inscriptions, and, observing that several of the amatory verses with which the prose narrative was interlarded were marked and underlined by my ancestor Daniel, signed by him, "Prithee, Mistress, read this as if I myself wrote it." Obviously Daniel had been in love with somebody, and, not himself a poet, had called on Sir Philip to speak for him. But who was his Mistress?

She was not far to seek, her name, written with an emphatic pressure of the pen in three or four places, was Mary Rondel. The handwriting was Daniel's, and the inference that it was Mary Rondel that he appealed to for his love's return, is irresistible.

Now this book had been given to my father in his boyhood by an old Miss Ingersill, his aunt; he had looked it over, no doubt as a boy, but he had stored it away out of sight ever since that period, so that in 1858, when the ghostly event occurred, he had not set eyes on it for at least forty years. Well, what of it? Why, this: that Mary Rondel was the name signed to several of the communications written down by Miss Ada Shepard at our séances in Florence in 1858. The communications stated that she had had relations with a member of the Hawthorne family about one hundred years before that date, and that she demanded the "sympathy" of Nathaniel Hawthorne, there present. But my father, thus adjured, had no recollection of the name of Mary Rondel, nor of any incident in the family annals such as Mary suggested.

Of course, I myself, a boy of twelve at the time, had never at that time seen the old copy of Sidney's "Arcadia," nor did I see it until nine years afterward. Ada Shepard never could have heard of or seen the book or the name until the moment when she first wrote the name down in the presence of the Brownings, and ourselves. I may add that Mary appeared, from the manner in which she would break in upon the mild discourse of the other spirits, and assert her rights to be heard in preference to them, to be a person of violent passions and dominant personality; she was, in fact, the only seemingly authentic communicant of them all. At that period, we always spoke of Mary Rondel as a veritable woman. How is it to be explained? We may guess and theorize, but it remains a curious problem.

My mother assiduously read many volumes on esoteric research, and she seemed to get comfort from

inhabited it—persons of the passing moment—whose activities were not overshadowed or controlled by influences from the past. The story, its scenery and ideas should be such as readers might recognize without straining their eyes into the shadows of early Colonial history.

Ten years before, when Hawthorne was engaged to be married to Sophia Peabody, and was casting about for a suitable habitation to take her to as his wife, he had considered throwing in his lot with the Brook Farm experiment. This was a sort of utopia, on what appeared to be a practical basis: persons of education and refinement, men and women, married or unmarried, with or without independent means, were to associate together in a self-supporting community; the men would raise market produce both for their own use and for sale in the neighboring city; the women would have charge of the household, and in their leisure do sewing and other women's work, for pleasure or profit.

It had no doubt been suggested by Fourier the Frenchman's remarkable writings on the Utopian theory; it was modified to suit New England notions of propriety; but common sense was strong in Nathaniel Hawthorne, and before taking a wife thither, he would test its possibilities as a bachelor. For a year or so, therefore, he put on ploughman's attire and dug and planted with the best of them. He made up his mind that the thing wouldn't work, and quit, married, rented the Old Manse in Concord, and dwelt in a paradise of his own, writing the tales that made up "Mosses from an Old Manse," helping his wife to cook dinner, and raising a daughter.

But that year in Brook Farm lived in his memory, and

when he needed a theme and place for his new novel, Brook Farm supplied them. Of course, the actual Brook Farm wouldn't serve. But "Blithedale" was the spiritual offspring of the reality, which gave substance to the writer's dream. The story is told in the first person by Coverdale, a young college graduate, with a leaning toward the romantic.

Beneath a tranquil and agreeable surface are latent powerful and tragic passions, disclosed only in the concluding chapters; the detail is charming, and the characters have unfailing human interest. Picturesqueness and simplicity are dominant everywhere, but the structure is strong, and the work is convincing throughout. Yet I doubt if "Blithedale" has had a tenth as many readers as has either of the two previous books.

The main incident of the book is the drowning of Zenobia; and in one of the journals of 1842 or '43, is a long account of the search in the Concord River for the body of a young woman of the town who had committed suicide by drowning. Hawthorne had taken part in this search, and his young friend George William Curtis was with him; the whole description is very powerful, and the essence of it appears in the book.

After the publication of "The House of the Seven Gables," in 1851, it was decided to move nearer to Boston; it was almost as far a journey to Berkshire then as it is to California now. One farm wagon carried our belongings, parents, children—one, a mountain-born baby a few months old—and Luther Butler, the farmer who drove us; but it was impossible to take the cats, seven of which had joined our outpost during the two years of our sojourn.

The farmer said he would take care of them; perhaps he did. They followed the wagon for a hundred yards, till the road dipped down the hill; looking back, we saw them sitting in a row, outlined against the sky. The woods that clothed the countryside were crimson and yellow; the air was pure, and the mountains surrounding the little lake—Stockbridge Bowl, as they called it—were gray in the misty morning sunlight; we would never see the like again.

"The Marble Faun"

JUST as the influence of New England produced "The Scarlet Letter" and Salem in particular gave the theme of "The House of the Seven Gables," so was it that Florence called forth "The Marble Faun." It was during his sojourn in Italy that Hawthorne conceived the idea of the humanization of the faun of classic legend.

The serious illness of his daughter Una with the so-called Roman fever (a malarial disease, often fatal), had caused him much and prolonged anxiety, and it gave him a sort of outlet for sad thoughts to play with this idea of the faun. It became a sort of anodyne, a deliverance from the pressure of forebodings in his mind. The ineradicable instinct for art came to his aid, and the rounded romance was the result.

Hawthorne was a writer and a poet though he wrote no verse. The rhythm of emotion permeates his romances. His works are art, and the art of literature had been his preoccupation all his life. In a degree, therefore, he had gained an insight into the other forms of art, and an understanding of their principles. So when he came in touch with the art of Rome, France, and England in painting, sculpture, and architecture, he could appreciate it and express his reactions. He got jaded in the interminable galleries, however, as he was not often wholly in sympathy with what he saw: this was not due to the technical demerits of the work he might be looking at, but to his own limitations of technical knowledge.

But for one antique statue in Rome, and for one painting, he felt unstinted admiration. In both cases, however, the thoughts and feelings they aroused in his mind rather than the work of the artists, moved him. The painting ascribed to Guido was the head of a girl, supposed to be Beatrice Cenci, on her way to execution; the statue was the figure of the Faun by Praxiteles. They touched Hawthorne profoundly; he made the statue his symbol in the story, and imagined a sisterhood between Beatrice and his Miriam. So one art received the others.

Hawthorne often visited the Capitoline Museum, and the Barberini, and pondered upon the statue and the painting. The problem of evil has been before him in all his stories from the first: Beatrice and the faun represented two sides of the mystery. In the legend, the girl had committed patricide, but for a cause that seemed to justify the act. The faun, on the other hand, was incapable of sin, because he was an animal not yet become human. Could the girl be forgiven? and could the faun become a man? Might not a story be written in which these two should be chief actors? The theme grew and put forth branches. It was worth attempting.

Except for the faun's pointed ears and tail, he was physically nearer man than animal. But he had never come under the rule of conscience; he was unable to discriminate between right and wrong; he was kindly and affectionate, but entirely unmoral.

Hawthorne assumed (for the end he had in view) that the beautiful creature, though it had no soul, yet might undergo experiences that would beget one in him. He might fall in love with a woman; but would love, as a faun loves, be enough? Of course, if the faun were mere animal, the quest would end there; but on Hawthorne's assumption of the germ in him of a soul, the outlook was better. And it was here that the thought of Beatrice came upon the stage.

As all who have read the book know, the faun for love of his mistress and to save her from the source of her trouble, a being who is associated with her as artist's model, commits murder. Sin and love combine to create manhood in him—to give him a soul. As the pressure of immensities dissolves rock into vapor, so the passion of that moment kindled the faun into a man. The delicacy with which the difficult theme is handled has its disadvantages. To keep the picture in harmony the artist is compelled to remove the whole scene with the characters that enact it into a region apart from reality, with the exception of Miriam, and of the faun at the moment when his crime is committed: none of the figures is convincing. But that moment on the brink of the Tarpeian Rock is rendered with a power almost intolerable, and it makes what precedes and follows, pallid by contrast.

The dramatic effect of the story suffers from the impossibility of solving the problem. The inference seems unavoidable that the story of the faun should have ended on the Tarpeian Rock. The rest is another story. And it is possible that Hawthorne, in his first vision of the tale, may have so intended, but then felt himself drawn on into the realm of consequences and did not resist the invitation.

Nathaniel Hawthorne's Prefaces

APROPOS of the familiar tone of his prefaces, Nathaniel Hawthorne says such mention of external habits, casual associates, and the like hides the man, instead of displaying him. "You must make quite another kind of inquest, and look through the whole range of his fictitious characters, good and evil, in order to detect any of his essential traits." And it is in the early tales that this inquest must be conducted.

In one place he calls these tales "attempts, and very imperfectly successful ones, to open an intercourse with the world." In other words, they contain Hawthorne's philosophy of life, speculations and conclusions upon matters vital to all mankind. They constitute, therefore, the corner-stone of his view of the problem of man, God, and the nature which is the medium between them.

Hawthorne was a radical in the profoundest sense of the term; but if he tests the pillars of the universe, he leaves them still apparently upholding the frame of things. In the story called "Earth's Holocaust," he turns, almost playfully, the seamy side of civilization to the light, but leaves no defect or absurdity untouched. In "The New Adam and Eve," he follows the wanderings of a new-created pair through the labyrinth of a great city, all the former inhabitants of the earth having been extirpated by some Divine decree; and their comments on what they find, and their perplexity over the traces of artificial usage, leave hardly anything worthy their approval except their own mutual love and their faith in a loving Creator; and these they did not find, but brought with them.

Again he pictures a respectable and blameless gentleman, a pillar of society and the state, who imprudently takes a peep into "Fancy's Show-Box." And therein he beholds himself guilty of every crime in the calendar; for though he had actually kept the Commandments, yet he had broken all of them in thought and impulse and been restrained from the act only by dread of consequences or by blind accident. In lighter vein, Hawthorne weighs the worth of things accounted precious in the world, and in the end finds all the treasures of the "Virtuoso's Collection" to be no better than rubbish. There is no cynicism here, however; if the worthless are exposed, the true jewels are revealed in their stead; no folly but may be retrieved.

It was not only on such matters that he applied his resources as a writer. In the little series of comments on "Old News," he takes up a bundle of newspapers of the seventeenth and eighteenth centuries. I think that these fragments of the latest intelligence of that far-off time must have been in the Hawthorne family for generations; for in some of his boyhood letters to his mother and sisters there are traces of their effect on his mind; and some of the earliest of his published sketches—as

"The Gray Champion," which opens the volume of "Twice Told Tales"—get their substance from such material. But in "Old News" he brings forward the tattered and yellowed sheets themselves, and by their aid pictures the scenes, figures, and customs among which they came into existence. The power of imagination to reconstruct the past and breathe life into it has never been more poignantly displayed.

It seems as if a writer who could make warm lifeblood run in the veins of a time long past, need seek no other field for his talent.

In the volume of "Biographical Sketches," Hawthorne proves himself a vivid and authentic historian, such as the best of English and American writers have never surpassed. But he was only trying his wings for what he held to be more important flights; he will not record merely, but create, though he creates even in recording.

Upon the whole these little volumes may be regarded as the cornerstone of his achievement as a writer. They abide at the base of the edifice, but the edifice could not have risen to upper air save on such support. There is little in the superstructure whose origins may not be detected in the productions of his youth and young manhood. And before sitting down to write "The Scarlet Letter" he had completed his forty-sixth year.

No one knows Hawthorne until he knows these books of shorter tales; and they justify the verdict that he was among the greatest of writers, whose product does not depend for its value on passing fashions, but is as sterling today as yesterday, and may still be valid in far-off times to come.

Translation of "The Great Stone Face"

SPEAKING of Longfellow and Hawthorne, I recall a curious incident, concerning a story by Hawthorne, and what happened to it.

Twenty years after the death of Hawthorne, Robert Carter was editor of *Appleton's Magazine*. He had been an admirer of Hawthorne, and had urged him to pursue the vein opened in the "Wonder-Book," and "Tanglewood Tales." Hawthorne died in 1864, and his books were still read. A manuscript story was submitted to Carter for publication: it was not well written, but it contained a striking idea, and Carter published it.

After I read the story, which had some such title as "The Profile on the Mountain," I called on Carter with a copy of Hawthorne's "Snow Image" volume in my hand.

The result of our deliberations was the discovery that Hawthorne's story "The Great Stone Face," had been discovered in a copy of the old New England periodical in which it first appeared, and had been translated into German by its finder and sold to a German magazine. There it had, in turn, been found by an American translator, and changed back into English—but not into the English that Hawthorne used. Sentence by sentence the two stories were the same, but word by word was all the difference that there is between India silk and cotton batting.

The German person, no doubt, had acted in good faith as a translator: the American had probably been unacquainted with Hawthorne's works, and thought he was introducing an interesting bit of German literature; and Carter had to blush because he hadn't known, or remembered, enough of Hawthorne to recognize the facts. The thing is a literary curiosity, and affords means for a study of style in literature which would benefit some of our young romancers of today. One might say that color and fragrance, tone and atmosphere, the music and magic of a master's use of language, are most of the game: a good idea badly dressed and presented is worth comparatively little. There is a legend that a Frenchman, putting into his own tongue Milton's "Hail, horrors!" came out with "Horreurs, comment vous portez-vous!" (Horrors, how do you do!)

Hawthorne, after more than thirty years of making a study of the writing art, could write in one of his prefaces: "In youth, men are apt to write more wisely than they really know or feel; and the remainder of life may be not idly spent in realizing and convincing themselves of the wisdom they uttered long ago. The truth that was only in the fancy then, may have since become a substance in the mind and heart!" Benjamin Disraeli, by the way, many years afterward, said the same thing in almost the same words in the introduction to one of his romances.

In the light of "The Scarlet Letter" and of the other two romances, the obscurity which had always attended the short stories and essays was deepened, by comparison at least. Not many could be induced to improve their acquaintance with them. And yet, not a little of the best that Hawthorne has done may be found in the pages of these little pieces. They are more finely wrought and deeply thought out than are all save a few passages of the longer tales.

There are, of course, a march, sweep, and resonance in the longer stories, and an emphasis and insistence upon their central themes, which make them easier to understand and digest. But in conception they are not finer. Hawthorne might have taken several of the ideas on which the "Twice Told Tales" and the "Mosses" are based, and expanded them into books which would have rivaled their fame. He had no encouragement to do this, however. He filed them down to the smallest compass, and made jewels of what might have been palaces.

The fact that he wrote not anonymously only, but under many different pseudonyms, kept him from recognition; faithfully though he worked for art, he continually worked against his popular and commercial interests. In a little tale, "The Ambitious Guest," he depicts his own predicament. The chief character in the story was possessed of a "high and abstracted ambition." He cared not for the wreath of glory that might be his during his lifetime; but would be content that, long after he was gone, the world should realize that the footsteps of genius had passed by. And in the short apologue of "David Swan," his young traveler lies down to sleep by the wayside; and during his slumber, fortune and success come near and would awaken him; but accident prevents, and he sleeps on unconscious. And in the preface of one of his books, Hawthorne remarks,

"I sat down by the wayside of life like a man under enchantment."

Mrs. Nathaniel Hawthorne
—Una Hawthorne

FAITH in God, such faith as brings angels who bear us up, lest we bruise our feet against the stones, was the faith my mother had from infancy, so that she hardly ever spoke of it, any more than of the shape of her nose. When her husband died, she wore black, not as mourning for his departure, but as a wedding garment for the immortal marriage with him that was to come—a bridal veil of a whiteness too dazzling for earth. As I have said, she was always conscious of his presence, and whether objectively or subjectively it skills not to ask; or perhaps we create what we feel.

This persuasion, or perception of hers, at any rate, may account for her strange willingness to leave his body in its New England grave, and put the ocean between it and herself. My mother and her children together would occasionally visit Sleepy Hollow cemetery, a lovely place in itself, and look at the white marble slab, and drop flowers there, but not tears. During their honeymoon in Concord, twenty years before, she and he would sometimes walk thither from the Old Manse, and plan to build a house on the very spot where his grave was afterward to be made.

And although he and she had planned together the

alterations and additions to the Wayside, the only home
of their own they had ever had, and had dwelt in it
long enough to make it seem a part of them, she didn't
regret leaving it, though knowing that we would never
return there. She never looked back, or down, but forward, and up. And yet, she was tender-hearted and
sensitive as an angel, with depths beyond sounding.

I was absent from her last earthly scene, but Una was
the guardian, and her story of it was preserved, and is a
fitting memorial of both mother and daughter. I have
never read another record so tenderly and condignly
true. It was drawn from a well of mutual love whose
springs are divine.

I have elsewhere tried to portray my two sisters, but
such labors of love are not always legible in common
daylight; there are regions of thought and feeling which
are never transcribed, and must be left to sympathy.
Una in her infancy, I was not in time to see, but persons more fortunate thought her adorable—a spirit
caught in its native fragrance but meshed on our mortal web for a season. This beauty never left her, though
when I first knew her, she being two years my elder, she
had begun to pass through a phase in which her inward
self was obscured, occasionally, by outward clouds—a
freckled little phiz, wayward tempers, and startling for-
ays into a queer maturity and hardness.

Her father and she were always in close alliance, and
his knowledge and imagination were constantly taxed
to interpret her. Una lived thirty-five years, dying in
England in 1879. Personal felicity for her was not in
her mortal destiny, and toward the end, she joined an
Anglican sisterhood, vowed to succor or console un-

fortunate women; she was not a Roman Catholic, as Rose was in her later life, though that seemed more probable for her than for Rose. Could she have been a writer, her troubles might have found an easier solution; but though she had the impulse and quality, she lacked the faculty that her father possessed; imagination could not temper her realities.

The man Una loved and was to marry died, so she stood bereft of both mother and beloved. Good women, thus destitute, are prone, in religious phraseology, to "seek consolation in Jesus." Una, with boundless energy and joy of existence in her, found nothing in this world to do or to be, and passed out to some better environment. A pale and frail nun she looked, lying on her pallet, in the cold, gray little room in the house of the sisterhood. She had an abounding sense of humor, too, but such a gift would fall flat on her worthy but meager companions. The telegram that she was in danger got to me too late; when I arrived at the door, a sister met me and said, "You are too late." It was an inclement day and I felt chilled and inert: I stood looking down at the body for a while, but could not even find any appropriate thoughts or memories. My sister was gone. If I had missed her, wanted her, loved her, this gray chamber was not the place for me to come to; wherever else she might be, she was not here.

PART SIX

Friends of Youth
and Later Life

The Tattler, and Algernon Swinburne

IN THE year 1879 I was living in London, and a friend of mine there was Robert E. Francillon, the novelist, author of many delectable stories, and a good fellow of the first water. He and I and some other enterprising spirits conspired together to establish a periodical, to be known—after Richard Steele's famous publication—as *The Tattler*. It was to be a weekly journal of literature, society, and of good things in general. It contained editorials, essays, reviews, and some pages of epigrams and paradoxes written by Halkett Lord, known in those days as one of the wittiest and best informed men in London.

But the grand *pièce de résistance* on which we counted for success was the manuscript of a serial novel by Algernon Charles Swinburne, which the enterprising editor had secured and which was good enough, and wise and humorous and witty enough, and more than interesting enough to make the fortune of any periodical—except for one drawback from which it suffered, which was that Algernon Charles Swinburne had taken it into his head that it would not do for him to allow it to be printed under his own name. When a poet, especially the greatest living English poet, takes a whim of this kind, it is worse than vain to attempt to dissuade him.

We could not judiciously tell him, as Guinevere told Lancelot, that it was his name alone that would conquer for us; he would have said that if we didn't think the story good enough to print, name or no name, we could send it back and go elsewhere.

No, it was to be printed, he insisted, if printed at all, under the name of Mrs. Horace Mann: though afterward, when we represented that a woman of that name already existed, the widow of a famous American educationist, and, in fact, an aunt of my own, the poet consented to so far modify the pseudonym as to make it Mrs. Horace Manners; and accordingly, this was the name finally printed on the title of the work when it appeared in *The Tattler*.

It ran its course for about six months, I think, in the columns of the periodical, and those who read it commended it highly: only, inasmuch as nobody had ever heard of a Mrs. Horace Manners, the great public was not drawn to purchase our *Tattler* in anywhere near such large numbers as would have been the case had it been known that we were running Swinburne as our novelist. The secret was only too well kept; and the poet, annoyed, perhaps, that British criticism did not rise as one man and proclaim Mrs. Horace Manners as the greatest living writer of prose fiction, declined, when the serial was done, to permit the story to be published in book form. It never was so published—and *The Tattler* itself, I regret to say, ceased to tattle after its first twelvemonth was up, being no doubt of an excellence in advance of its epoch: and the whole episode passed into oblivion. But of course the numbers of the paper were enshrined in the British Museum Library, and the fact that Mrs. Horace Manners was Algernon Charles Swinburne did finally transpire, and was recorded in literary catalogues.

But in truth, the novel, entitled "A Year's Letters," is one which no author need fear to father or mother, though Swinburne never officially lifted the mask from Mrs. Horace Manners. I say "officially" because, as you now know, the secret became an open one.

The letters of which the serial novel was composed are written by each of the characters of the story, as was done long before in Smollett's "Humphry Clinker." The predominant personage is a wise old woman of the world, everybody else's grandmother, mentor, and friend, who might have sat for the portrait of the charming old lady of one of the last of Du Maurier's cartoons in *Punch*. Does any one remember her?

The elderly captain is making his call on her and is hesitatingly drawing from his dexter pocket a yellow paper-covered volume. "I've brought you a book to read, grandma," he says, "but it's French, you know; and I don't know whether it's quite—quite—" And the kind old lady, with no illusions, holds out her hand. "My dear boy, I'm ninety-six years old, and I think I'll risk it!" Such an old lady, admirably presented, is the presiding spirit of "A Year's Letters." It was Swinburne's first novel, but "Love's Cross Currents" is often mistakenly asserted as such.

Ellery Channing

I NEVER saw either Ellery Channing or Thoreau at the Emerson conferences. The former had become almost as much a hermit as the latter. Thoreau, though, had once or twice lectured at the Concord Town Hall, and was respected but not popular. Channing had passed through various phases but shunned the public eye. He was firmly built but not tall; his features were strong and serious, his eyes habitually downcast as he walked the streets; his speech was gruff and monosyllabic.

The American Channings seem to have begun in Newport, Rhode Island, and were distinguished from the start. Edwin Tyrrel Channing and his brother William Ellery Channing were well educated, refined, courteous; the first reaction from the primitive Calvinist of the prime; not yet too pragmatic and skeptical, but "broad" and conversational. They were born not more than a decade or so after the close of the Revolution. None of the Channings ever had gold, except of the kind that is not subject to rot, robbery, or moths. With wealth of spirit they were well endowed, and William Ellery Channing spent his share of this wealth generously. He was held to be the father of American Unitarianism and was the first to expound that doctrine from the Boston pulpit.

I was about to say something of Ellery, cousin or nephew of Ellery Channing of post-Revolutionary days. He was held to be an enigma. His friends agreed upon calling him "Ellery," to mark, I suppose, his divergence from the predominant traits of the Channing stock, most salient of which, in that pious age, was his unconcealed discontent with religious dogmas in general. Tristram Shandy said that the British army swore terribly in Flanders. Ellery made a point of doing the same in Massachusetts; but he did it in an historic way, when other people were there to hear him; I doubt whether he was at the pains to swear to himself in solitude. In other words, I fancy he was not so much an infidel as a doubter, indulging in profanity by way of discouraging religious conversation in advance. He was possessed of obstinacy and weakness, a combination which often makes an interesting character; and interesting he was, if sometimes tiresome in his wilful perversities. He turned for succor to art and poetry, saying that all in Christianity that was really sane and worth while was derived from paganism.

Ellery was a man of moods; he was emotional and variable, one man today and another tomorrow, or the next hour; but he became increasingly gloomy and reserved as he grew older. He assumed to ignore and despise society but was really of very social tendencies, though he covered timidity with roughness. His powers of self-control were limited; he delighted in making himself incomprehensible and was angry because nobody understood him.

He married rather early in life, his wife being a sister of Margaret Fuller. She was clever and attractive but wearisomely selfish. She and Ellery made a tortuous and jolty life of it; he was passionately in love with her at intervals, and fought with her fiercely at other times. Soon after their marriage Margaret Fuller wrote to my mother suggesting that Ellery and his wife, who were casting about for a habitation, should lodge and board with the Hawthornes in the Old Manse in Concord, which the latter were occupying in their honeymoon years.

The indelicacy of such a proposition would have been obvious to anybody but Margaret and her sister. Hawthorne replied in a letter which is quoted in my biography, "Hawthorne and His Wife," and is a masterpiece of its kind: courteous, kindly, but explicit; studious in avoiding injury to the sensibilities of the persons concerned; lightened with humor here and there, and enriched with imaginative touches. Margaret and her sister never forgave it. Ellery himself saw the point and was silent; though years afterward, in a whimsical mood, he allowed himself to say silly things about Hawthorne.

Some one remarked of him, foolishly, "The only person who can tame Ellery is Sophia Hawthorne." "Tame" him, forsooth; he was but a grown-up baby. He conceived causeless dislikes of people and embarrassing affections; he clung to poor Mr. Tappan, for instance, like a lovesick leech, refusing to take hints or even kicks, till Tappan, to be quit of him, had to fly to Europe. That he was related to the great Channing may have helped unbalance him. At last he abjured society and turned sullen. Most extraordinary of his eccentricities, perhaps, is the fact that for an inordinate length of years—fifteen or twenty, I think—he dwelt under the same roof with Frank Sanborn. With all their virtues, these two men were the most impossible to live with, yet never a ripple disturbed the peace of their companionship.

Clara Louise Kellogg

I WAS always in love as far back as I can remember, though not always with real girls; poetry-girls often cost me delicious torments. Sitting beside that brook at the foot of our lawn or skating alone on Walden, I would give rein to my transcendental passions. I was in love with that Huguenot maiden that Millais painted, and with an old engraving of the Duchess in our copy of "Don Quixote." I could use such as these as basis for divagations into what Shelley calls the "intense inane," but there is in real girls something that anchors you to reality, and the loveliest flesh-and-blood reality is not plastic enough for the free soul. A moment will come when you don't love them so much and you drift elsewhere. This applies, though, to boy-love only, which demands the Infinite in the Particular. By and by you become practical and take the best you can get. Picture-and-poetry girls, being products of human imagination, yield to lovers' changes.

Then, too, boys bashful in the presence of real girls— as all worth-while lovers are—keep their secret, and so suffer their imperial votaress to pass on, in maiden meditation, fancy-free. But they can avow their inmost emotions to the unrealities without blush or reservation.

231

I am sure none of our Concord schoolgirls knew that
I was in love with them, and I could play the invisible
Don Juan to my heart's content. If there was here and
there another, who didn't happen to be in the school,
that was my own affair. I am faithful to those memories,
and reverent of them. I reverenced them, as their spirits,
could they be recalled to testify, would affirm. I thought
of love as preluding marriage, and of a kiss as betrothal.

Actresses and singers, however, occupied a special
domain, allied to pictures and poetry. They were not
real because, as I knew them, they were always not
themselves, but imaginary. So I could be in love, at the
same time, with Charlotte Cushman and Clara Kellogg,
and with half a dozen more: it was always their impersonations, not themselves. If this reasonable distinction
were more often observed, our young stage-door aspir-
ants would escape much trouble. Don't mistake Juliet
or Lady Teazle for the honest lady who earns a livelihood by reciting their lines. You won't get Juliet, and
you don't want the honest young woman. Observe, too,
that not all actresses are behind the footlights, or even
on the silver screen. Nor need romance involve scandal.
Married people in old New England who found
themselves cooling a little toward each other might find
a redeeming warmth in being at home, and so fall in
love on a new basis. Parlor, library, bedroom, attic, cel-
lar, barn, kitchen—their associations become a larger
human character, assuage present disagreements with
memories of former felicities. The spiritual interweaves
with the material, and substantiates it; one sees com-
pensations and recognizes extenuations.

And speaking of Clara Louise Kellogg, James T. Fields who had so solicitously taken me to William Warren for my Buckingham costume, also took me to see and hear Clara. She was an angular, awkward little thing, but with dark eyes and a voice of flexible enchantment, and with amazing self-possession. Fields and her other promoters might have doubts of her success, but she had none: her stage walk was preposterous —a monstrous prance—and she knew nothing of stagecraft, but her voice overflowed all imperfections as the clear tides of ocean submerge with their bright translucence the rocks and inequalities below; when we heard it, we knew that a new joy had come into the world; for the voice of every great singer seems to outdo all precedent.

The opera was "Faust"; and when, halfway through, the audience wanted a certain passage over again, and the orchestra began something else, Marguerite broke off being Marguerite, and walked down to the footlights as Clara, and told the conductor his mistake; then went back into Marguerite once more and finished the encore. "My stars!" whispered Charlotte Cushman, then a veteran of thirty years' standing, "I wish I had such courage!" After the performance I was conducted behind the scenes and presented to Clara, still in her Marguerite attire.

I was so obviously in love both with her and with her rôle that she smiled and went to her dressing-table and gave me a carte-de-visite photograph of herself in the jewel scene, when she is partly disrobed. Disrobing was not then what it might be now. But the little photograph meant everything to me, and I still had it when she and I were more than forty, and I called on her in her New York hotel. She weighed one hundred and eighty pounds, but her eyes were as beautiful as in her girlhood; her face was a work of art; she was nervous and restless; she recalled perfectly our meeting a generation ago, she said, and told me she had retired from the stage; and my Clara-Marguerite was no more.

Boyhood Memories of Drury Lane
—Edwin Booth

AS I THINK of the masked ball which that great actor William Warren made such a success for me, when he accoutered me as Lord Buckingham from his vast wardrobe of theatrical costumes, a few of those who could claim the right to put on such raiment, arise before me.

From the time I sat as a small boy in front of a vast green curtain which glimmered, waved, and wrinkled mysteriously, suspended between two worlds, the drama has meant much to me. That first performance was the Christmas pantomime in the year 1856. It was entitled "The Grasshoppers' Feast and the Butterflies' Ball." Historic Drury Lane Theatre was packed to see it, and when the great green curtain came down and the palpitating hour was over—after Titania, with a wave of her magic wand, had overcome all obstacles, until at last, the lovers became a prince and princess, and Clown and Pantaloon shrank back into the old toad and his mate, to be lost in the glory of a sparkling Paradise—the small boy was himself again: but never quite the same small boy, "for he on honeydew had fed, and drunk the milk of Paradise."

Not until after several years on the western side of the Atlantic did the boy, no longer small, again await the rising of the green curtain. The auditorium was as vast and as populous as before, and perhaps the boy was almost as tremulous with anticipation; but the crowd around him were Bostonians, unprejudiced, but un-impassioned. However, the Boston Theatre seldom disappointed its patrons, and the public was favorably disposed toward the younger son of the famous Junius Brutus Booth. He had been on the stage since his sixteenth year, though little known as yet, in Boston. So they laid aside their volumes of the essays of Emerson and the sermons of Channing, and were assembled to deliver their verdict on the young man's performance of Sir Edward Mortimer in "The Iron Chest."

Of the adventures of Sir Edward Mortimer I recall little; but I fell at once under the sway of his impersonator, a slender, graceful youth, with great melancholy black eyes and poetic hair, and a voice whose sweetness and power were irresistible. Edwin Booth was what we term "magnetic" from the first; we might dissent from his interpretation of a part, but in his presence we never rebelled, with that voice of a thousand tones caressing us.

No audience would have too much of his Hamlet; at first it was a revelation, and it grew to be our idea of Booth himself. From time to time he would introduce minor variations; coming on the scene for the soliloquy, for instance, he came forward as if unseeing, or seeing more than was in heaven or earth, and stumbled unawares upon the armchair which happened to be in the center of the stage, and, after reassuring himself of its reality, sat down in it. He told me he was constantly studying the part and getting fresh conceptions, thereby, of course, relieving the strain of the innumerable "runs" which the public demanded of him. A purblind tyranny! Both the part and the audience would have profited by other impersonations.

Though Booth was older in years, we were close friends, and he was never old. On his fiftieth birthday he said to me, "I feel like a giddy boy!" When it came to a hundred, a thousand, repetitions in succession, of "Hamlet," he had need of youthful powers. "Half the time," he admitted, "I go through it in a dream, or mechanically." It was a great refreshment to him to act a play with Salvini or with Irving; though it might be questionable policy to put two great artists in the same play.

In "Othello," "Julius Caesar," and a few other plays, he and the other would alternate the chief parts; and with Salvini, it was interesting but queer to hear each speaking his own language. And even Irving's English seemed alien beside the American's. But Irving was not more distinguished than distinct—great in his own way: though Disraeli, seeing him on the stage for the first time, in the late 1870's, said he was "a third-rate actor." But Disraeli, though himself a supreme actor, was not a competent critic of professionals. "Has it not been well acted?" murmured the dying Augustus twenty centuries before. And Shakespeare (in a mood) assented: "All the world's a stage!" And Poe, in another mood, affirmed, "The play is the tragedy, 'Man,' and its Hero the Conqueror Worm!" But come, gentlemen, it is at best but a half-truth. As the man of the Elizabethan era wrote on the front of his house in Chester, England, "They say and they say—let them be saying!"

Booth as we know had to kick against the pricks; first, that hereditary craving for liquor. The good and lovely woman he married in his youth knelt beside him every night, praying with him that he might overcome it. She died, and dark was his despair. He married again, but the mind of his second wife began to totter, and Booth was in torture. By good fortune, she too died, leaving him shaken, but still with his genius and charm. He had outlived the Lincoln assassination, and might still be the idol of the multitude. He was to welcome Irving to New York, and he and Irving and Bram Stoker and I would sit in an upper room of the hotel, and I could have listened to those three till dawn. But at last Bram and I would convey our beloved Edwin home in a cab and leave him in the affectionate hands of his servitors.

Fanny Kemble
—Edward A. Sothern

AMONG others who were worthy to wear the historic costumes in that collection of William Warren's, was Fanny Kemble—after divorcing Pierce Butler she resumed her maiden name, and came to live near us in

Lenox for a time, while my father was writing "The House of Seven Gables."

She was a heroic woman, in beauty as well as in character: she had pulled her brother, Charles Kemble, the actor, out of his money troubles by giving Shakespearean readings; she acted in England, too, for a time, and wrote several books—reminiscences, plays, criticisms, and poems. She used to come riding up to our little red cottage on her great black charger (this was in 1851) and one day, as I stood gaping up at her, she stooped and seized me by the belt and lifted me up before her on the saddle; off we galloped, wheeled about and returned. She held me out at arm's length: "Take your son—Julian the apostate!"

Unlike Charlotte Cushman, she carried the stage about her in private life, and my mother told how, going into a dry-goods shop to buy a yard of cloth, she frightened the clerk by pointing to a defect in it, with a tragic gesture, and—"Yet there's a spot!" She was robust and ruddy. She didn't put on the dramatic style for effect; it was natural to her, being of a dramatic family.

Booth, shy and modest though he was, could not divest himself of the buskined style; but he had been on the stage so early that I suppose he had no style of his own. Stage people varied in this respect, but you could generally detect actors or actresses by their enunciation; they didn't mumble and clutter up their words, but treated them with respect.

It was an education to converse with Ellen Terry— if you could sufficiently protect yourself from the assault of her overwhelming temperament, from her matchless, sparkling, sensuous charm to pay attention to her speech. Her long association with Henry Irving was not more surprising in other ways than in the fact that neither of them adopted anything from the other—they stimulated each other to keep their highest level.

I enjoyed the great comedians of that time; there was a good number of them, and they were consummate artists. Comedy was perhaps more artificial than tragedy, and the working out of the details was delightful to observe. William Warren was with the Boston Museum Company, which was a group of such talents as was not elsewhere to be seen, nor has since then been collected.

Sometimes a star from other regions would come to the Museum for a season; one of them was Lester Wallack, the handsomest man that ever stepped on a stage, and perfect in his parts.

Edward Sothern—I mean Edward Askew Sothern—was the delight of mankind while he lasted; and when he died, halfway through his fifties, there was none to replace him. When Tom Taylor had written "Our American Cousin," he had named Dundreary among the dramatis personae, to be sure; but his lordship had no more importance in the play than the flunky who announces the carriage. Taylor's knowledge of the type was hardly skin-deep; but, when, in a fortunate hour, Sothern was picked to play it, the young actor had the purse of Fortunatus in his grasp. No two characters could be more unlike than were Sothern and Dundreary, but the one immediately knew the other to the marrow, and made him bloom and put forth roots till the rest of the drama became but a negligible vehicle for him; the plant burst the flowerpot. The entire character is made up of Sothern's "gags"; the others do but minister to his joyous idiocy.

239

As I look back, it seems to me that I have left untouched half of what I had to say. The twilight is deep, but the shapes that people it do not fade to my eyes, now that I have become accustomed to renewing their environment.

Thinking of those jovial meetings with Irving, Bram Stoker, and the beloved Booth, so often in his cups, recalls another drinking scene—if such it can be called—at the Wayside long ago. In Hawthorne's tower was a secret cupboard, wherein were preserved for some great occasion two bottles of priceless wine, presented to my mother by the King of Portugal, when she spent six months there in 1854: and now, the great Occasion having arrived, I was commissioned to go to the closet and fetch the bottles. I put them on the table reverently, and my father opened one, and the cork came out in a way which brought to his face an expression of anxiety; he put a thimbleful of the vintage into a glass and tasted it, and looked up at my mother and said, "Sophia" (he always called her that in public), "I'm afraid there has been a mistake!" After our distinguished guests had gone, there was an investigation, and it transpired that Belinda, our cook, recently dismissed for inebriety, little as we then suspected the real cause of it, had drunk the contents. And the tragedy was that she would have preferred gin. After emptying them, she filled the bottles with dishwater.

Wendell Phillips

AS I have said, chief among Concord entertainments
was the Lyceum Lecture Season. Lecturers have in-
creased in numbers during the last fifty or sixty years,
but not in quality. College professors, with a few British
recruits, are giving us much information, but not often
presented with the art that makes it intelligible, because
of poor enunciation, and mumbled words. This dearth of
elocution is due to the decease of trained actors and
of the legitimate drama, "movies" and "talkies" being
the executioners. We don't resent this because this is a
new generation, which never heard or saw the real
thing, and as Othello would say, don't know that they
are robbed. It is easier to deprave than to elevate, and
this depravity is spreading, so that our college undergraduates and our next-door neighbors utter words
without heads and tails. The prospect is that human
speech is getting outmoded, and we are reverting to
animal or Neanderthal methods.

Long ago the Children of Israel despoiled the Egyp-
tians of their goods; but one would rather lose one's
purse than one's tongue. In Concord Town Hall in the
1860's elocution was at its apogee. The persons who
stood up before us on the platform were good to see and
hear: the intonations and enunciations of an Emerson,

a Henry Ward Beecher, a George William Curtis, promoted civilization, apart from what message they might bring.

We were expert judges, for we knew the Kembles, Keans, Booths, Cushmans, Ristoris—all the trained performers of the great tragedies, comedies, melodramas; and such humorists as William Warren could be artists even in farce. Humor is a half-divine gift to man; when humor flops over into vulgarity or near obscenity, we may laugh, but between that and real humor the difference is as between an angel's smile and the snicker of goblins.

Among those famous orators in the Concord Lyceum, was one who seemed to be heaven-gifted—Wendell Phillips. He was the very flesh and bone of educated New England, Boston-born, Harvard-trained. Garrison had antislavery views, but nobody could compete with Phillips in melodiously enthralling and infuriating a mixed audience. He was a blond, slight-built man of mild aspect; but when his eyes began to sparkle, he was an army with banners. Nothing more delighted him than did a mob thirsting for his blood, to whom he was as a summer breeze bearing deadly pestilence. Anybody could have thrashed him, but he was so destitute of the ability to feel afraid that a self-appointed bodyguard of young fighters followed him about and sat on the platform, as avid for the opposition's gore as these could be to string our Wendell up to the lamp-post. George Smalley, one of the Phillips bravos, who was long afterward the London correspondent of Greeley's *New York Tribune,* used to relate to me stirring incidents of the warfare, which I was not fortunate enough to witness myself. George, even in peaceful London, looked more

like a professional bruiser than Tom Cribb and Tom
Sayers did, but was a good writer and observer, and had
a lovely wife who helped him through in society.

When war broke out, Phillips' chief aim was no
longer pressing, and he subsided into social converse or
addresses on subjects of general interest. One of his
favorite themes was the story of Toussaint L'Ouverture,
the Negro liberator of Santo Domingo. How gallantly
he told it! You seemed to see him riding beside Toussaint at the head of the men who marched for freedom
or for death. "In arms!" he cried, with a kindling smile.
"Marching in arms!" And the peaceful audience that
sat beneath him in Concord Town Hall stirred and
vibrated at the challenge, and loved the Negroes more
than ever.

The last time I saw him was at a reception in the
house of George L. Stearns, father of my faithful Frank:
a nice place if they would only let you alone more. This
time they had two show guests, Emerson and Wendell
Phillips, who, standing apart from the others, were exchanging a few remarks. Mrs. Stearns vigilantly spotted
them and emitted a gush of remonstrance; she was a
rather large maternal woman, and came upon the two
lean philosophers, full-bosomed, as upon fugitive babes.
"Now, this will never do! Here we all are famishing for
your words of wisdom, and you go off to whisper to
each other in a corner!"

Phillips, and Emerson, too, for that matter, could
face a mob, but this was a more trying predicament. All
they could do was to smile foolishly and falter some
platitude. If people may be killed by kindness, why
should overkind persons be allowed to live? On the con

trary you can't help loving them, even after such a scene as I have portrayed.

William Cullen Bryant

A REVEREND personage was William Cullen Bryant, of a temperament serene but chilly, like his autumnal "Waterfowl." He was as ancient as Alcott, and almost wrote "Thanatopsis" in his cradle. In Harvard, in my freshman year, I passed two undergraduates crossing Harvard Green, chanting some verses in unison, and I caught the words "join the innumerable caravan"—already a classic after half a century, but no longer, I think likely to be quoted by undergraduates (even Harvard ones) as they stroll through the Yard. As the English would say, it simply isn't done any more. But "Thanatopsis" isn't forgotten, and the stripling in his teens who composed it, and didn't himself realize how great it was, kept on mounting toward national and world-wide visibility till he became, in the mere routine of the day's work, a national and honorable figure.

Though that personal chilliness couldn't be thawed out of him, everybody—especially women—liked him; he was a straight-out New Englander, severe but never malignant, and years and renown couldn't weaken that tough fiber. He was good to look at, too—a bony six-footer with a superb head, covered, as I remember him, with a great bush of snow-white hair: a steady dark eye, and a Roman profile; somebody made a bust of him at

JULIAN HAWTHORNE
at sixty-nine with Frances Biglow Davis, niece of Lowell
(Lowell's old home, Mass.)

that period but not adequate. He was editing a powerful political newspaper, and (as a pastime, in his late seventies) translating the Iliad of Homer.

He was physically efficient too, to the last, doing his "setting-up" exercises every morning, and, on one snow-bound morning that happens to be of record, actually tramping through drifts and ice from his office on lower Broadway to pay his New Year's calls on his amazed friends in Fifth Avenue. He smilingly pooh-poohed the ladies' exclamations, as he brushed the snow from his boots in the hall: "A winter-day tramp does good to a man!" He was not a poet of love-lyrics, but I should have liked to see him pounding out his resounding hexameters from the Greek. Homer captivates robust poets in their old age, as well as such super-craftsmen as Alexander Pope; Tennyson transferred one noble passage into English; and it was a pity that he was lured away to the Arthurian story. But that was the ingrained English of him: he couldn't emancipate himself from Victoria and Albert, and the British worship of British royalty, even when it bore a German accent. Of course, he might have done worse—and he did, sometimes.

In these years only one other man in New England could rival Bryant in splendor of wavy hair and beard —Henry Wadsworth Longfellow; and Longfellow was the handsomer of the two. In youth he had had a voluminous and poetically wavy growth on his crown, but shaved his cheeks and chin—a mistake, for his lower face was weak; in his later time he remedied that, and really justified his best poetry. But he never affected the careless splendor of Bryant: he was trimmed and pomaded, and he wore the latest fashions in coats and trousers, with lustrous boots and a gold-headed cane; it was invigorating to see him stepping down the street, with his cordial smile.

A generation later, hawk-nosed and black-haired Mark Twain, having established his literary reputation, suddenly, like a black-boughed apple-tree after a snow-storm, bloomed out like a snow image; not only his clothes, but his hair was in almost spectacular tumult, though jaws and chin remained shaven: he seemed brighter, and happier in spirit, too, as well he might, having won his fortune by grim hard work. Toward the end, though, he seems to have missed cues with the dogma of personal immortality: a sad lapse for a humorist, but humorists, I think, are not seldom prone to it. Like Omar, they suspect God of playing a practical joke on Creation. But their doubt is honest, and Tennyson said that there lives more faith in honest doubt than in half the creeds.

Henry Wadsworth Longfellow

LONGFELLOW, in my memory—that is, during the last thirty years of his life—was always perfectly clad, and even in his old age held to the ideal. One usually saw him in a snug-fitting sack coat of dark cloth and lighter-hued trousers: a collar and scarf, with a jeweled scarfpin, the envy of every Harvard undergraduate: shoes spotless and lustrous, gloves, and a silk hat.

The whole figure was trim and trained as a West Pointer's: and the head was superb. The beard was not long and stringy, but all curls and vitality, and the hair of his head was abundant and hyacinthine. There is a bust of the Greek Sophocles for which he might have posed.

But the expression was of glowing, sympathetic amenity, radiating happiness and good will to man: his ready smile brightened the day. He looked like a good man, prosperous, the most popular and loved poet in New England and he was precisely all that. He had outlived the physical frailty of his youth: he was married to a lovely woman whom he ardently loved: he had charming children: he dwelt in the pleasantest old house in Cambridge. Life was beneficent to him: he was honored by his peers.

But life was not to leave him unchiseled by grief. One of his children died. The loss cast a shadow over him, but it was transparent, and he found a beauty in it which was reflected in his poetry. But there was to be a later tragedy, too poignant for poetry, and the blow fell suddenly without warning.

It was on an autumn or early spring day, 1867 or '68, with sunshine, yet cool enough for a fire in the open grate. Longfellow and his wife were together in the tranquil room, with the prospect before them of tranquil years of ripened marriage love; they had always been lovers. The woman, passing before the grate, was all at once in flames. Her skirt had caught fire by a draft of air from the open window. Her husband sprang to her and tried to brush out the fire with his hands, which were severely burned: but the flames leaped upward and could not be quenched. To her, the injuries were fatal. The horror of the experience to a man of Longfellow's tender sensibilities seemed intolerable.

But, aided, I suppose, by religious faith and by his temperament, the poet survived. He was at this time engaged upon his translation of Dante's "Divina Commedia" which was begun in 1867 and finished in 1870. The poem is a stern one, but its lofty imagination may have helped to comfort him. Interspersed between the cantos of the poem are sonnets which he wrote during his work, and among them is some of his finest verse. They made no direct allusion to his loss, but there is an organ note in some of them that is absent from his earlier product. For, be his absolute stature in poetry what you like, he was in his degree a true poet, whose life inevitably declared itself in verse. His intuition for the right word and rhythm was marvelous, and so effortless that the reader is affected, he knows not why: the simplicity and straightforwardness amount to genius.

In 1853 he went to England, to remain there seven years. In 1855 appeared Longfellow's "Hiawatha": the fruit of his studies of the Indian legends. The poem, in book form, appeared immediately in London and was for several months the staple stock-in-trade of British reviewers. The form and versification were so unusual that there was a prevailing tendency to ridicule the work: and Henry Bright, a dear English friend of my father's, fell into the habit of putting his private letters into Hiawathan verse, entertaining us both by the latter and by himself.

Hawthorne, however, was far from sharing the current English opinion of the poem; he insisted that it would outlast most English and American poetry of the day, and he read it from beginning to end to our family circle in the evenings at our little villa in Rock Park, across the river Mersey from his office in the

Liverpool consulate. It had an immense success with the Hawthorne children, who spoke in Hiawathan terms long afterward: and time has confirmed Hawthorne's judgment, and even the English skeptics have long since repented. As I regard it now, it seems to me one of the most original and satisfactory achievements in verse of the century. Its force and fire are unabated from start to finish, and it is fresh and hearty as a spring morning.

There was gentle dignity and eloquence in almost all of Longfellow's later writings. After Hawthorne came back to Concord in 1860, Longfellow would occasionally venture so far: but he never cared for transcendentalism or its professors, and could not find congenial companionship in Emerson and Alcott. With Hawthorne, he was always at his best: but he would rather entertain him in Cambridge, or surprise him in some rare visit to the Old Corner Bookstore on Washington and School streets, than invade his Wayside privacy.

For men of such widely differing type, their friendship and liking for each other were remarkable.

A Beacon Hill Episode

WE MET no obstacle in disposing of the Wayside—after due consultation with Mr. Stillman, the family lawyer. He had been one of the earliest friends of our family, dating from the Old Manse days, and seeing Una in her lovely babyhood. But when it was proposed to name her Una, after Spenser's heroine, he demurred, because, lovely though her babyhood was, her after life might deviate from the line of perfection. However, the young mother scorned the aspersion, and the infant was named Una.

Stillman formed polite friendships with men of letters here and abroad, and collectors of a future age, browsing in his bookshelves, must have found rich clover. Neatness and order were indispensable in his demure Pinckney Street household, hushed, so patrician, so lifeless—even the books on the neatly arranged shelves bore lids of leather, to protect the tops of them from dust. Mrs. Stillman was as little noisy and aggressive as any other schooled city mouse, but whispered, not squeaked; her only occupation seemed to be that of tatting; and the cook and housemaid were too well selected to need direction. The latter I never saw; the cook was a powerful and vital Irishwoman, whose cooking was beyond rivalry.

The household routine in Pinckney Street had no variation or shadow of turning; as it had been, so it was and must ever be. No ripples on the surface, no lapse from elegance and propriety; no disagreements nor surprises. The breakfast-table was ready for business at 7:59. At eight the door opened, and the husband was in his chair, with a gracious matutinal gesture, unfolding his newspaper. At five minutes before nine the spouse stood noiselessly in the door with ebony cane with the gold head, and anon, the office and law volumes.

Thus had it been for forty years! On a morning following that, Mrs. Stillman was in her place, and was about to handle the coffee-pot when she noticed beside her plate a sheet of note-paper, neatly folded and addressed to herself in Mr. Stillman's chirography.

I have hitherto been idling among these details, because I am reluctant to pull the string which transforms diverting comedy into stark tragedy. The little missive itself, which the lady is now to read has not survived, but a summary was sent to me in London:

My Dear Ursula: You have been suitably provided for in my Will, and the Pinckney Street house is yours for life. [Did this portend suicide? The poor lady's hand must have trembled. No, not suicide, but much worse!]

Norah [the cook] and I, have removed to a lodging in Cambridge Street and will live there for the rest of my life. She is the best cook in Boston, and in herself a desirable woman, such as I have longed for always and never before found. After your first agitation subsides, you will become sensible of the advantages of the new arrangement. I beg you will make no effort to alter my decision, which is irrevocable. Your conduct had ever been irreproachable, and though social opinion will condemn me, I feel that I am making the best recompense in my power for half a century of error.

Akin to these were the words that met the startled eyes of the punctilious, fastidious, and invariable Ursula Stillman, the pink of propriety of Beacon Hill.

In spite of his request, every pressure was employed to overcome this intolerable situation. The man and his cook stuck together until, some two years later, he died, well cooked-for and serene to the last. Respect and sympathy for the wife were universal, and he was unanimously condemned—except possibly in a secluded corner of some club, toward midnight, after the waiter had brought the last drinks and retired for the night.

Then—a toast to the hero who had defied Beacon Hill and got away with it! There are kinds and degrees of courage, but seldom arises a man to die, free, after seventy years of bondage to respectability, in the arms of his chosen cook. Nature and temperament, and the world well lost!

A novelist of the period describes a character which must have been Stillman under the name of Amos McGentle—"a grandfatherly greyhound on its hind-legs." Stillman was rather tall, thin, closely buttoned up in an old-fashioned body-coat, with mild wise eyes, straight nose, mouth and chin short, in proportion to the development above. In conversation, he had a way of bringing together the fastidious tips of his long, delicate fingers, and he would arch the right eyebrow with a subdued suggestion as of perceiving the absurdity of the Universe, but too cultured and courteous for open laughter.

After these threescore years, nobody can be harmed, and many may be edified, by the recounting of this tale, a strange story, at first hardly credible, but appearing at last as an instance of poetical justice, with justice on the side of mercy and recompense.

A Tennyson Incident—Bayard Taylor

ANOTHER anecdote about Tennyson—we see him and an English friend somewhere in France. Neither French-speaking, but muddling through as Britishers best can. Tennyson had a terrific cold; French hotel rooms are unsympathetic; but a trivial fire was finally made to splutter in the travelers' bedchamber, and the poet, huddled in his black cloak, cowered over it, while his friend sallied forth on some unavoidable errand. But the waiter (or bedroom steward), was first summoned, and an effort made to set him on guard in spite of alien tongues. "Foo!" said the friend, pointing toward his snuffling companion: *"Non—laissez—sortir!"* The waiter, a veteran of the Revolution, comprehends perfectly, and planted himself outside the door in a dauntless attitude. Minutes ticked away; suddenly the door was flung open, and Tennyson plunged out. A personal engagement ensued, resolute on the veteran's part, rapidly becoming furious on the poet's. The friend's return, barely in time, prevented fatalities— berserker rage against Gallic fidelity. "What—what is this?" Tennyson foaming at the lips, essays to explain: "I wanted to go next door; this miserable frog-eating menial won't let me!"

The Frenchman, panting but resolute, avouches his

stainless honor in an outpouring of vocabulary which may be thus interpreted: "You, monsieur, warned me that this monsieur, being insane, must not be permitted to escape. *Parbleu,* we have struggled—and—*voilà!*" "But all I told you was, not to let the fire go out!"

There is much to be said in favor of Volapük.

Bayard Taylor turned up one day at the Wayside, with his Moslem beard and sociable eye: the aroma of far lands always about him, the grace of a paladin, the renown of strange travel, of romance in print and fact: it was he who composed the "Bedouin Song," still quoted in "selections":

> From the Desert I come to thee,
>   On a stallion shod with fire,
> And the winds are left behind
>   In the speed of my desire.
> Under thy window I stand,
>   And the midnight hears my cry:
> I love thee, I love but thee,
>   With a love that shall not die
>   Till the sun grows cold,
>   And the stars are old,
>   And the leaves of the Judgment Book unfold!

I have always held that to be the real stuff, and marveled how it could have come from the same pen that committed "Hannah Thurston," and I know not what other prose calamities.

Bayard, at this visit, told us that he had latterly been giving lectures on his adventures, and that he was recently back from a voyage to the West Indies in a sailing ship; my mother said that she had made that voyage when she was a girl and had cured herself of seasickness on the stormy trip by making the captain fasten a rope to the mainmast—she lying on a mattress on deck —and hauling herself erect by it; the grasp on something stable in the whirl and plunge of chaos having restored her faith. Bayard admired; but had no better rejoinder than that he had beguiled his journey by reading the several volumes of a new poem that had just come out—"The Ring and the Book," by Browning.

"You read it all?" my mother asked, wondering.

"Every syllable!" declared he. "But then, you know, the trip lasted nearly a month."

"And how did you like it?"

Bayard stroked his beard, and replied: "If a man says anything, he's sure to say a good thing before he's done; but really the thing wasn't so bad. And I think it toned me up to do some stuff of my own: Fields is going to print them in the *Atlantic*."

I read them afterwards, in the exclusive periodical, and wished our friend had never written anything other than those and the "Bedouin Song." He himself remarked that they seemed to flow out from him without effort; but probably Browning would have said the same of his "Ring and the Book" in four volumes—or was it six? Poets never can tell when they're off the track—at any rate, Browning couldn't.

Bayard Taylor—only in this respect like the Father of Lies—never wearied of going up and down in the earth; and I remember, when I first saw him in boyhood, and was told that he had been in the land where Abraham came from, I looked at his shoes, as he sat in our parlor, and thrilled at the thought that they had trodden in the footsteps of Abraham.

Henry Morford

THROUGH some untraceable links of thought the name of Henry Morford becomes visible to me through the obscurity of years. He had appealed not a little to my liking and sympathy. He was upon the whole a pathetic figure, for his idea of himself was that he was one of the great personages of his age: that he moved in a continuous splendor of purpose and of achievement.

His imagination was portentous—he was obsessed by it, and actual events made small impression upon him in comparison with the vivid colors and grandiose forms that his fancy and expectation painted. He dwelt in palaces and sat on thrones. Only toward the last came a gradual and grievous awakening, and for a short unhappy while he recognized facts.

We were introduced to each other at some public dinner in New York, and I saw a superb face and figure of a man perhaps five and thirty years of age, with the bearing of a prince. His attire was the conventional evening-dress, but it seemed somehow more splendid, either because it was so nobly worn, or from some touch of fancy in the facings or the waistcoat, or it might be merely from the glow of the red rose in his buttonhole.

We fraternized as members of the literary profession. He was an Irishman, of kingly lineage, but proud to unite himself with our glorious American democracy —but I must visit him at his place. He must make me known to Mrs. Morford—"and until you know my wife, you don't know me!" The mate of such a man must be princesslike; and her consort and I forthwith agreed upon a day and hour, and I was impatient during the three-day interval.

"My place," he had said: and I visioned a broad estate, with an imposing mansion in the midst of it, approached by a winding drive through the shade of lofty trees and the velvet green of spacious lawns. To be sure, he had mentioned a street number in the environment of Brooklyn; but I had spent a good part of my youth in England, and knew less of Brooklyn than I was to learn later. That Morford was a man of great wealth, inherited rather than acquired, I doubted not—his carriage, speech, and manner demanded it—and I wished I had a brougham of my own, to make a suitable entrance into his domains. But probably a suitable vehicle would be awaiting me at the gates. The weather was fine—early winter: I gave unusual attention to my toilet, remembering that princesses are sometimes critical; the ferry landed me in Brooklyn, and I began my quest for the "place"; but the street named surprised me; it was narrow, devious, and with affiliations in the direction of the waterfront; the number—why, here was the same array of numerals, but obviously there must be some radical error: this dingy and battered little portal in a crowded tenement district could bear no relation to my king of men: I must enquire and seek further. But after fifteen minutes of painful vagabondage I found myself facing the same impossible door. And in desperation I mounted the three dirty steps and pulled at a bell-handle. Perhaps a dark corridor would lead me magically into the wide-extending private park containing my objective.

A step that shook the small frame house sounded in the passageway, and the door was flung wide; a man in shirt-sleeves, with hospitable hands outstretched, was welcoming me and drawing me inward; that flashing eye, that bearded front, those heroic shoulders—by Allah, 'twas no other than Morford's self! Ere I could draw breath I was staggering down a darkness terminating in another doorway, a bit ajar: through that I plunged into a fifteen-by-eighteen bedchamber, which was also kitchen, dining, and living room!

The bed, with its parti-colored quilt, and feather pillows, and four wooden-bottomed chairs, one weak in the off leg, partly veiled by the folds of the green flannel dressing-gown thrown over it; the gilt china vases on the mantelpiece, and above it the framed photograph of Mr. and Mrs. Morford in the wedding finery of five years before; the four-burner range with the pots all a-going and the princess stirring one of them as we came in, but turning with a wide, frank smile at—"Here he is, Molly, my love! Your hand to our honored guest, sweetheart!"—and had I had the fortune to be Irish myself, bedad if I'm not after thinking I'd have bussed her then and there and got away with it! For a princess she was of rosy, hearty, deep-bosomed County Kerry womanhood.

Eyes dancing under her silky black eyebrows, small hands and shapely, if a bit roughened by wifely domestic chores; a foot for Cinderella, which as she came toward me got entangled in a hole in the rag carpet, so that she all but threw herself willy-nilly into my arms.

Oh, her husband needed no broad acres and stately mansion—she was wealth enough. But it would take a Thackeray at his best to depict that ménage and the dear people that lived in it. Fragrant memories of that leg of mutton with caper sauce come back to me across the gulf of more than half a century.

George William Curtis

GEORGE WILLIAM CURTIS, born in 1824, was in the prime of his manhood in the 1860's. He was a friendly, cultivated, charming person, seeking and finding beauty in man and nature, and cultivating it in himself. It is difficult to picture him as anything but cultured in his cradle. In his teens, I believe, he had begun his career as a clerk in a business office, where, I fancy, he was the object of adoration by the females of his environment, and was hated by his fellow employees. Whether to escape from the attentions of the former, or from the jealousies of the latter, he quitted that scene betimes and appeared, while still in his twenties, in the famous community of Brook Farm. There he stayed long enough to make the acquaintance of George Ripley, Emerson, Hawthorne, and Margaret Fuller, and got himself a manly physique and sound health: then he went abroad for four years and investigated Europe and the East; wrote "Nile Notes of a Howadji" and was known thereafter to his friends as

"The Howadji." Had they translated the term into "Globe Trotter," which was all it meant, he would, I think, have been cruelly wounded.

Curtis was an acceptable lecturer on the lyceum platform in Concord, where he was the Admirable Crichton of attire, elocution, grace, and complacency, while the moral tone of his addresses, and their edifying substance and (when the Civil War and slavery were the theme) his infallible adherence to the Higher Thought, were all beyond cavil. Later, he was to bolt the Republican party and become the first mugwump, and it showed no small moral valor in him to endure that nickname with seeming equanimity, though I'm sure he never sullied his own chaste lips with it.

But in truth he had sturdy pith in him, and was a gentleman *sans peur et sans reproche,* holding righteous opinions and proclaiming them boldly, even when he didn't happen to please the unregenerate. He was generally liked, and he knew personally most of the men of eminence of his day. The word "slogan" as at present used and worn to a frazzle, was unknown then; but had it been, "Sweetness and Light" would have been his.

What was his costume at Brook Farm, I am not informed, but I can hardly imagine him in shirt-sleeves, not to speak of overalls: no, he must always have worn that exquisitely fitting body-coat, those immaculate trousers, that adorable necktie, that ring and those shiny boots; and have always appeared freshly shaved as to mouth and chin, with only those carefully trimmed side-whiskers. Did he wear kid gloves and a silk top-hat? He did! He was born, like Minerva from the head of Jove, full panoplied in such things. A psychologic student would find a worthy subject in this person: how could a human being so infallibly and fathomlessly nice, at the same time possess courage and stamina enough to defy, fight, and overcome the embattled political rascality and corruption of his age, without once condescending to raise his mellifluous voice, to make an indecorous gesture, or stick out an aggressive jaw? He hit the line hard, and he made his goal, but always with a bow and a smile, and a "Pardon me, gentlemen, for exterminating you!"

Curtis was a modern gentleman of the old-gentleman school, to teach ornament rather than building. Because he was an old friend of our family, I always went to hear him lecture: faithfully though I attended them, as I might pore over my brook, for its music and picturesqueness, I didn't bring home many nourishing fish from them. He would pose for his hour, in his faultless apparel, tranquil hands hanging folded in front of him, the glimmer of a smile on his lips, turning page after page of his manuscript on the desk; retire at last with a courteous bow. Who could image such a person immersed in the sweat and mire of the public arena? His polite essays in *Harper's Magazine* "Easy-Chair" were mere moralized chitchat; his novels were society gossip. Yet there was something beneath all that, and when Boss Tweed's era began, Curtis turned back his shirt-sleeves and became a mugwump. Hitherto he had breathed perfumes only; but the stench of civic license drove him to protect his educated nostrils by downright fisticuffs. The surprised public, then as always mixing credulity with skepticism, first grinned, then sobered. Much aided by the heavy slugging of Tom

Nast, down at last went Tweed and his gang, and the possibility of the gentleman in politics was established.

To have lived in this world sixty years, in the public eye without fear and without reproach, is no small achievement. Curtis did that and more: he schooled and disciplined himself to conformity with a highly civilized ideal, and he sought and improved means to make his fellow man as good as he was. He had his vanities, his complacencies; greater men have had them too, and for men less than great they may be necessary to keep them up to their activities. The fact that George William Curtis doesn't loom larger than he does to a later generation is due, perhaps, to a lack of tangible ruggedness in him, of indignant emphasis, of original force. I don't know that he ever expressed strong religious convictions; perhaps that cost him temporal immortality.

Charlotte Cushman—Ristori

CHARLOTTE CUSHMAN had come to us from London when I was a small shaver, in the 1850's; she was magnificent in silken attire, but simple and genial in soul as the Boston girl which she used to be. My first serious love-madness was for her. I never got over that passion, and was amazed and indignant to read in a biographical paragraph on her, long afterward, that she was a homely woman! I got out my photographs of her: well, of course a photograph never does one justice; but what of her Lady Macbeth and Rosalind, and didn't she create "Meg Merrilies"?

Her nose wasn't classic, perhaps, but there was a power and splendor in her countenance that took captive your soul. In the magic art of acting none was higher.

After we had heard Clara Louise Kellogg together, she gave me tickets for her "Meg Merrilies." Her entrance at the back of the stage was terrible indeed; nothing else could compare with it, then or since. Tattered, with long gray hair streaming past her shoulders, barefooted, stepping as light as a deer. That wonderful face, those awful eyes! And as those eyes fell upon the man whom, since his childhood, she sought—he was sitting at a table in the front of the scene talking with another man, and sipping beer from a flagon—she recognized him after twenty years, and halted on one foot, pointing with her left hand, the other clutching her ragged staff. When would the fellow turn and meet that appalling gaze? Not until the suspense had grown intolerable, and the two thousand spectators choked for breath: Meg, meanwhile, motionless as if Gorgon-smitten. I don't remember the incident in Walter Scott's story, but I see her poised there in mid-flight, hovering, intent, ghastly, as plainly as I first saw her— how long was it ago?—eight and sixty years! Charlotte Cushman invented—created—that scene, and none other has dared attempt it. And she could do Romeo, too.

I asked Edwin Booth, who was of course the very Romeo of Shakespeare, whether he ever found an adequate Juliet to act with him. He thought awhile, and shook his head with a sigh: "Never one that both looked the part and could act it." No: one or two were pretty enough; and Julia Marlowe understood the part, but she was, and looked, old enough to be Juliet's mother, and did the balcony scene with a maternal air. Modjeska could achieve a delicate beauty; but Juliet was not a Pole—and her "Heest, Rromeo, heest!" curdled our blood.

Great actors and actresses seldom have good support, not always through their own fault. Booth was utterly irresistible as Petruchio, but his Katharina was absurd—a vacuity.

Henry Irving began the realistic-scenery fad, and Beerbohm Tree overdid it, and audiences were progressively corrupted. And actors try (at best) to act up to the scenery but rarely make us forget it. In Shakespeare's time, they would hang up a notice, "This is Rome" or "This is the Forest of Arden," and the audience would catch the idea, and be left free to enjoy the performance, which in that crude age was supposed to be what they had come for.

I remember there were private theatricals in 1854, in London, with Minnie Warren and me in the cast; we did "The Beauty and the Beast," and Minnie was the Beauty and I was the Beast, doubling for one of the ugly sisters. We took it seriously; I had the whole play by heart and did the prompting for the others. Ten years afterward, we acted plays of a more mature kind at Sanborn's school, and in "Ici On Parle Français" I was the paterfamilias, Lily Nelson my wife, and Wilkie James the Frenchman. Wilkie was beyond praise, and I was so fascinated in observing him, that I utterly forgot my part in the most important scene. So I gave up the ambition to become a great actor; but I still considered the project of being a great preacher, like Henry Ward Beecher, or Spurgeon. I thought it would be nice to join Livingstone and be an explorer in Africa; and this resulted in determining me on being a civil engineer and building Brooklyn Bridges. The one thing I resolved never to be was a writer.

But to return to scenes of high drama. Salvini's great countrywoman, Ristori, had come to us years before, bringing her own company with her. An extraordinary catastrophe occurred at her performance of Lady Macbeth at the Boston Theatre. What was the matter with her leading man, Thane? We hoped he had been taken suddenly ill only; but in the dagger scene we began to fear something inconceivable on the Boston Theatre stage. His knees sagged, his feet stumbled, his voice whined and blurred; he seemed about to collapse, and Lady Macbeth was obliged not only to take the daggers, but to hold her spouse up by his neck gear while she lectured him. The scene was cut short, and the sinful Thane didn't appear again at all, and the play ended with the bloodspot on Lady Macbeth's hand. The audience was painfully interested, but it neither laughed nor hissed, but applauded Ristori emphatically. She had proved herself great as both actress and woman.

Ella Wheeler Wilcox

INTERMITTENTLY, through the years, it has been my fortune to come upon Ella Wheeler Wilcox, and when I last saw her, about 1914, her beautiful brown eyes were even clearer and softer than when I had seen her ten years before. She admitted to me that she was a Theosophist, and that she was glad to be among the disciples of that remarkable faith with its depth and power.

There is no one to my thinking among American women who deservedly stood higher in the regard of the people than did Ella Wheeler Wilcox. Her name and her work have been familiar to the public throughout the years, and they can bear witness that no word she has written in prose or in verse, and nothing that she has done or attempted, but has had the best good of her fellow creatures in view. But even she herself could have but a partial conception of the truth she has demonstrated to the doubting, of the assurance of warm human affection that she has brought to those who had felt the hardness of the world.

Though all she said was in illustration of a deep and universal philosophy, which, in its full exposition, would justify the ways of God to man, yet, there was always a personal touch in it, so that each reader felt it in his private consciousness, and as a word spoken for his intimate ear.

And no one who has had the privilege of looking into her face could doubt that there could be no sinner or castaway who could fail of finding, in her, understanding and compassion. Her warfare against evil was ceaseless and unsparing, but she condemned no human victim of evil.

Those who knew her best know that her voyage had not been over summer seas. No one who has read her works could doubt that she suffered as only a woman of spiritual depth and sensitiveness could suffer.

I have often heard her spoken of as a "brilliant woman." But brilliance implies a hardness of surface reflecting light. I would be better content to call her luminous, with a light that warms no less than it defines.

I recall her saying that "we cannot crush back our propensities, untried, into ourselves; we must let them curb themselves by experience of their consequences." She also gave utterance to a noteworthy thought on marriage. She was talking of a young woman she knew who was working enthusiastically in literature and journalism. "But," she added, "she never married. She perhaps fears the burdens and restraints of marriage. But every wholesome woman wants to marry, and should marry. It would be better for a woman to be divorced three or four times, than never be married at all."

What a full, beneficent life was hers! What results to be produced without extrinsic aids, by the independent growth and activity of a generous, human, truth-seeking and truth-telling nature!

She had loved life, had found love in it, and had dispensed love; yet she did not feel regret at the thought of the end of life here. "When one begins to understand," she told me, "there is nothing terrible or unnatural in death. Only one would like to go at the same time with those one loves."

Jacob Riis

AS THE caravan of men who have made their mark in the world passes before me, it is with pleasure that I linger upon the achievements of Jacob Riis. He was a

267

berserker, and possessed no small endowment of sacred rage which made his ancestors dreaded. He was a fellow countryman of Hamlet the Dane; but, unlike that melancholy Dane, he seemed to be uniformly in capital spirits.

He was born in 1849 in a little Danish village by the water. His mother was brought up in the castle where the ghost was wont to walk. He lived in Copenhagen, but emigrated to America about 1870, and save for short visits to his home remained here. In his book "The Making of an American" he tells how an American, in his own proper person, was made. It is most delightful reading from beginning to end, full of instruction and full of events and adventures and strung on the golden thread of a charming love-story (a true one, in fact), which had then passed its silver anniversary, without mishap: the wife who had given him several children, American-born, was to him "my silver Bride."

Mr. Riis was the intimate friend and energetic fellow-worker of Theodore Roosevelt, then President of the United States, who found in him a man of strenuousness not inferior to his own; and, between them, they made things move in New York.

Jacob Riis was a man unknown and unregarded, with not an atom of pull outside of his own personal strength and faith and indignation against evil, a foreigner with an accent that led to his being called "The Dutchman"; with no particular education beyond what a schoolboy gets; bred a carpenter, and shoved into a newspaper office by necessity—by the pinch of hunger and general destitution; a man far from pliant or conciliating, much more disposed to be aggressive and dogmatic, with bitter prejudices, in spite of a wonderful faculty for admitting that he had been wrong, when he was shown to be so to his own satisfaction; a young fellow wholly without experience of the great world. Sticking to a few fundamental principles and making them tell in the end against the whole embattled host of corruption and trickery; constantly defeated and disappointed, yet never giving up or disheartened, and finally, victorious all along the line, ridiculed, but resolute; narrow perhaps, but with an edge on him like a Damascus blade. This man, with such odds against him, personal and circumstantial—doing his work in New York exclusively, and in a small district of New York, and largely unaided, or getting aid only after he had laid, by himself, the foundations of success—made himself a national, and even an international figure, and at fifty-two was recognized as one of the leading heroes of genuine municipal reform.

It was an extraordinary fact, of most welcome augury, and outweighed any quantity of negative things and evil tendencies; it shows the ability of the affirmative and fighting soul against the false and perverted one. The book that brings all this before us may rightly be called a great book, and journalism may be proud that it was written by a journalist, and indicates how measureless a power for good journalism, rightly used, may be.

Never was there a franker autobiography than "The Making of an American." Mr. Riis has no disguises; he is transparent; he is always thoroughly abreast of himself, permitting himself no arrears, no morbid reticences, no secret grudges. There was another brilliant volume put forth by another great journalist, Mr. James

Creelman; in that we were shown the kingdoms of the world and the splendor of them, the great men of the earth in crucial moments of their careers. It was a cosmopolitan book if ever there was one, "On the Great Highway," and illustrated what journalism is in its more august aspects. But Riis's book is not less great and remarkable in a totally different vein with subject matter diverse from the other as the poles.

Sir Richard Burton

FROM time to time I take down a volume of the "Arabian Nights," and meander amusedly through its remarkable tales, for the translation of which we owe a debt to Sir Richard Burton. It is pleasant to think of such a man; indeed there never was just such another, though, if he must be classified, I would list him with Laurence Oliphant and Edward Trelawny.

Burton had two lives, both of absorbing interest to men and women: one, his career as an explorer, the other his love affair with Lady Burton. He was of the type of Englishman which justifies the opinion that the English entertain of themselves; they are extremely rare, but they do exist and they are undeniably English.

He was born in Hertfordshire at Barham House in 1821 and died in Trieste in 1890. During most of his active career abroad, he was consul in one place or another; though I imagine there was never another consul so independent and unconventional as he. He began life as an officer in the Indian army, but got through with that phase about the time he was thirty and, casting about for something pleasant and therefore dangerous, bethought himself to make the journey to Mecca.

No European could enter Mecca and live: that was the main attraction; incidentally it would be interesting to see what they had there. He went into training for the rôle of a Mohammedan, and turned out so excellent an article that he deceived the very elect, and, with only a few adventures that would turn a man's hair white, got safely out again, and told the tale—told it well, for he had among so many other gifts the literary gift as well.

The next thing that attracted him was Africa, at that time a Dark Continent in the full meaning of the word. Livingstone had been in Africa about fourteen years and was there still; Burton, however, attached himself to John Hanning Speke, and remained there most of the time for the next seven years. He discovered Lake Tanganyika, and made the ascent of the peak of Camerun. Any out-of-the-way place suited him; he visited South America, Damascus, and I know not what other remote places. He was the prototype of the men in Kipling's ballad, who have it in their blood every year to "go away from here"; nothing could keep him long amidst the tameness of civilization: not even the love he undoubtedly felt for the woman who wooed and married him.

As soon as she was safely his wife, she naturally accompanied him in his travels; she was as remarkable in her way as he was in his; but she was unlike him in being exceedingly religious and in some respects fastidious; we all remember how she burned his manuscripts on the ground that they were not proper to print; un-

271

doubtedly they were not proper; but one cannot avoid unregenerate longings.

He was knighted in 1885. He mastered thirty-five languages. His literal translation of the "Arabian Nights," in ten volumes, was published in 1885–88; of this his wife issued an expurgated edition.

Thinking of this notable man, I am reminded of a notable event—utterly unaccountable. The strange scene, which took place in the Philippines, never reached us through the newspapers, the censor deciding that it was "not news, but poetry." It was at Malolos, and Funston, with the Kansas regiment, was in trenches, facing the Filipinos. The band had been playing some dance music, when of a sudden, to the astonishment of all, there came from the enemy's lines the sound of the hymn, "Stand Up for Jesus." It was thought to be a ruse to induce the Americans to expose themselves, but when the music had ceased there came from the insurgent camp a rolling throb of drums, and the band swung grandly into "The Star-Spangled Banner."

There was a moment of surprise, and then the whole Kansas regiment, stretched out for near half a mile, leaped from the trenches and stood on top of the earthworks. Every soldier drew his heels together, uncovered, and placed his hat over his left breast. It was the regular salute to the national anthem. There they remained straight and motionless while the enemy continued to play the one supreme psalm of America. The whole line was exposed. Not a man carried his weapon, yet not a shot was fired.

John Ruskin

THE newspapers made him seventy-five at his death, but John Ruskin was born in February, 1819, and therefore had all but reached his eighty-first birthday when he died. The great age of so frail-looking a being reminds one of what the lover in Tennyson's "Maud" says of the sea shell: "Frail, but of force to withstand . . . the shock of cataract seas that snap the three-decker's oaken spine!" Ruskin indeed, like Swift, began to die at the top: and this sometimes prolongs life in the case of sober and intellectual men by diminishing the wear and tear on the physical machine.

The day of his earthly career was a day of days, with an ambiguous dawn, a glorious morning, a splendid noon; then clouds, often beautiful, began to fly irregularly over the face of the slow-declining sun, and it set at last in gray shadows. But all through the journey there had been strange happenings: fairy portents; illusions of vapor; openings through the vault into heaven itself; mutterings from the abyss; passionate storms that drove all before them in whirling rout; exquisite chantings of fairy music sounding from haunted forest; joyous psalming as of cherubim and seraphim beholding the countenance of the Almighty; and again, sad accents of almost despair, as of a soul who saw Eden lost, with no hope of returning.

Perhaps, however, you would prefer to have your Ruskin described unimaginatively, in good set terms. But all such attempts would be incongruous, and set you further from the truth than ever. What I felt most distinctly about him was that he was unlike other men, not in intellect so much as in nature. He was queer; looking him in the eyes, you saw light, inspiration, insight, fancy, fanaticism, genius, and the incarnation of all these things, and more like them. But what you did not see was the incarnation of a normal, natural man or woman. Male nor female was he, but something of another genius altogether, as we might suppose an inhabitant of Mars or Mercury would be could he visit us. Some impassioned and companionless elf, left over after the others departed, together with faith and belief and the sense of justice, and other good lost things; seeing with the intensity of a fairy our lacks and misfortunes, and zealous to cure and reform us; weaving marvelous spells of words and paces to that end, but finding always a stolid wall of selfishness and blindness resisting all efforts either to scale it or to trample it down. And yet there is little doubt that the world of art, of morals, and even of political economy would have been in worse plight than they are had Ruskin never lived.

The only serious mistakes he made, were when he tried to enter personally as a fellow creature into the life about him. There was the transcendental absurdity of his marriage, for example. The idea of Ruskin posing as a domestic character is one of the jests of the ages. A woman, one would think, would as soon undertake to become the wife of a perfume, a cloud, a metaphysical abstraction, a wandering zephyr, a ray of moonlight, a bit of blue sky, as of him. There was fire in him—abundance of it—but not of the sort that warms the family hearthstone.

Whosoever would seek to thaw his fingers over the flames of a will-o'-the-wisp might hopefully expect husband comforts from Ruskin. Nevertheless he did marry with the result that the world knows. He had a tongue which could, like the fiddle of the youth in the fairy tale, "draw water from a stone, or milk out of a maiden's breast that bairn had never known." He was a bodiless intellect, a disincarnate emotion. I remember seeing him coming along the pavement of Piccadilly. He drifted from side to side of the pavement, with his eyes seeing things invisible.

In his faded brown clothes he resembled an autumnal leaf, blown hither and thither by a light breeze. He was not like a person. Had I walked straight at him I should have passed through him, neither of us feeling anything. But what a vast power he was always in his thoughts and writings! They stand like the adamant and will endure for ages. But what other people and he himself seldom or never understood was that in order that Ruskin should remain Ruskin and be potent for good and truth, you must let him alone, not try to establish familiar or personal relations with him.

Coventry Patmore has a verse in point. Speaking of a rainbow which he vainly tried to overtake in his childhood, he draws the moral, "With whatsoever's lovely, know it is not ours. Stand off to see; or beauty's apparition so puts on invisibility." The rainbow and Ruskin are glorious when you accept them for what they are, and let them do their appointed work in their proper manner.

Count Leo Tolstoy—Nikola Tesla

I HAVE read much of the writings of the great reformer and philosopher, Count Leo Tolstoy, the man who felt the possibility of putting into practice the precepts of Christ.

The grandeur of Tolstoy's position is well known. He was as much a dreamer as a philosopher, but the changes he desired were, for the most part, as undesirable as they were impossible. He was the one man in modern times who aimed to live as the Savior seemed to him to command, yet he was greeted by his own countrymen with the harshest and narrowest bigotry.

Perhaps if those who blamed Tolstoy for his too literal Christianity could have seen his surroundings, they might have comprehended the stages by which he arrived at his point of view. Undoubtedly he was both honest and sane. Even in the harshest periods of his austere life, he seemed to be happy.

No one familiar with the facts could doubt that, however erratic his course, he aroused the thinking people of Russia to a partial sense of the social, industrial, and political iniquities against which his peasant life was a standing protest. Tolstoy never gave up his idea that physical labor was a duty imposed on every man: and that he would continue to his dying day to plough in the field and to make shoes, no matter what society might say. The secret of his life was love and labor.

He worked four hours every day with his pen, but he also did his stint of manual toil. He went out among the downtrodden peasants, not only to preach the holiness of labor, but to share with them the satisfaction and dignity of producing wealth with his own hands. Imagine Shakespeare, or Goethe, or Dante, or Victor Hugo, or Thackeray leading such a crusade in his declining years!

The thought of Tolstoy, his wife and daughters, his environment and his habits and his idiosyncrasies, is powerful and impressive, but all is subordinated to the spiritual lesson of his unique career.

Thinking of spiritual men makes me recall the figure of Pope Leo XIII. There was immeasurable spiritual power, existing in a man feeble and fragile in age, when I saw him—destitute of all earthly power and property, and isolated from all the human race, in the recesses of a cloister, for at that time the Pope was not permitted to go beyond the confines of the papal estate.

Yet there he was representing spiritual power over millions, coexisting with the extreme of physical powerlessness. The White Shepherd of Christendom sitting remote and solitary in the Vatican, and yet, his word and his thought were heard and heeded to the uttermost parts of the earth. The Pope expressed his belief that Christianity alone is capable of composing the troubles and discords of this world: and he believed that he, as the vicar of God upon earth, was the chosen medium of peace.

I could not but make a mental contrast, when I saw the gorgeous officers of the church, the imposing guards that watch over the Pope, and pictured the vast array of superb and historic apartments through which access is obtained to the presence—and then, at last, nothing but the simple old man in white, with his delicate ethereal face and his kindling eyes, and his distinct melodious voice.

Nikola Tesla falls within the category of spiritual men, to my way of thinking. His insight into things electrical is unique among men. But he does not stop there, for I recall his comments on art, which are good to recall. He affirmed that it was impossible for any artist to paint such a picture as the Sistine Madonna of Raphael. Raphael let himself be absorbed in his picture. "He is swallowed up in it. He disappears," he said. "You can find no trace of the man Raphael there. But in the pictures of a man like Sargent you see Sargent throughout them. He writes himself, in every picture. You see the power he has had to look into his subject's mind and drag forth his secrets, and set them down on canvas." Tesla declared that to be the way of the present age. The great artist can no longer obliterate himself in his work. It is his individuality that shows clearest. He possesses his subject. He is not possessed by it.

This is true criticism, and Tesla's implication was that the highest results of abstract science can be reached only by those who make a surrender of themselves similar to that of the artist Raphael, and his great contemporaries. Tesla is still busy with his inventions, and I believe he will not die until he accomplishes what he was sent here to do. If he does, no man will ever have served his fellow men to better purpose.

Henry Ward Beecher

HENRY WARD BEECHER at the height of his renown was a great foursquare beef of a man, with an intellect, and dauntless—that was all we knew of him, before that entanglement, concerning which public opinion has been divided, then and since.

He had been in England and defied fashionable political opinion; but why should such a man choose the pulpit to express himself? What an admiral he would have made, or general, or leader in Congress, or President of the United States! He would have carried the Free-Soilers to victory. In the light thrown upon him by the sentimental interlude which caused the great scandal, it seems that the sensual instinct in him, inseparable in such big creatures from their other bigness, determined him to religion, as bringing him into closer touch with human nature, male and female. Luther and Melanchthon were both great exhorters, but it was the author of "Wein, Weib und Gesang" who changed the face of the world. The annals of the monks of the Middle Ages would never pass the Boston censors. Perhaps the most powerful pulpit-thumpers of all ages were prone to be full-orbed and complete. We can't trust hearsay.

Henry Ward Beecher would square his shoulders,

plant himself on both feet, and every eye was upon him. But he wouldn't get away from himself—not then and there. He could murmur as a cooing dove, as well as bellow like a bull of Bashan. In such a man's companionship, men would feel liberated, and women might feel that the boundaries between human and divine love might be less impassable than they had been taught to believe. The boundaries of the Whole Duty of Man?—Henry Ward Beecher, preaching in Plymouth Church, Brooklyn, drew a vaster congregation than has ever since assembled there, and the great scandal trial could not discourage it.

Sometimes, elsewhere, he dropped religion from his theme, but he held his audience. One Sunday I conducted my friend Robert Ingersoll, the famous agnostic, and his two young daughters (one of them pretty) to hear Beecher preach. We sat in the front row; neither of the girls had ever before attended church. Beecher, addressing the offspring of the notorious disbeliever, thundered and warbled his finest, and after the service stepped down to ask them how they liked it. The pretty daughter declared, with enthusiasm, that it was just like going to the theater! Her father, a trifle embarrassed, smiled and cleared his throat; Henry was delighted. "Come again!" he told her, looking into her eyes and holding her hand tenderly. Give him a chance and he'd convert her!

Beecher was born at Litchfield, Connecticut, June 24, 1813, was graduated from Amherst College, then preached for some years at Indianapolis before becoming the first pastor of Plymouth Congregational Church. On the breaking out of the Civil War, his church raised and equipped a volunteer regiment. At the close of the war, Beecher became an earnest advocate of reconciliation.

When he preached, he practically ignored formal creeds, but set forth what he believed to be the gospel of Christ, and he loudly denounced slavery. He wrote many lectures and papers on religion, which appeared at first in journals of the day, and later in journals in which he was financially interested. He even tried his hand at writing a novel, but it was poor stuff.

His sister Harriet, who married Prof. C. E. Stowe, didn't go into the pulpit or the lyceum; but she captured millions with "Uncle Tom's Cabin," not a little to her own surprise. She was a little, homely wisp of a woman, but with a fascination. She was far from being a genius: it was Abolition that sold her story. Her subsequent novels were flubdub. Stowe was rather dry, and not unaware of the awkwardness of husbanding a woman more important than himself.

The Byron scandal happening to be resurgent at that time, Harriet went into it with ardor. It wasn't correct form, in the 1860's, to call by name such idiosyncrasies as adultery and incest, but discussion could be managed. The poet must be guilty; Byron was dead, but his widow might be cross-questioned. So Harriet took passage to England and contrived an introduction to Lady Byron, and before long that poor old lady was telling all she knew.

Happening to come back on the same steamer with my mother, Harriet unloaded her whole precious cargo. My mother could, of course, adduce no evidence in rebuttal; but the good Lord has ways of protecting such persons. Byron had an overwhelming imagination, and could make a fiction out of himself. "Thou shalt not bear false witness against thy neighbor"; and the best way with evil report is to let it pass out of the other ear. Harriet was fain to carry her wares to the printer. My father, I should suppose, looked up under his dark brows from the book he was reading, made a movement of distaste with his shoulders and said nothing. But it didn't take Harriet long to write all she had heard from Lady Byron's lips.

PART SEVEN

Recalling
Some Books and Happenings

Bettina von Arnim
—Alfred Henry Lewis

I REMEMBER reading, years ago, a book written in English by Bettina von Arnim, who in her girlhood was a pet of Goethe's, and sustained incomprehensible relations towards him, whereof the most incomprehensible feature was that they seem to have been innocent. Her book was a sort of reminiscent rhapsody, like nothing else ever put on paper. In a species of delighted trances she recalled episode after episode of their intercourse, relating the most absurd or extraordinary things in the most naïve and unrestrained manner.

Bettina was only a very young girl at the time of her infatuation, which makes her story more than usually strange. She addressed Goethe as a god, and pictured herself as his absolute worshiper, yet retaining a singular liberty of criticism and comment, which came like a tinge of lemon juice on the sweetness.

The book was illustrated with outline drawings by herself—and she knew as much about drawing as she did about writing, which was nothing at all; and moreover she had never learned the English language, but got it up out of a dictionary as she went along. But the fascination of the book was incomparable; it magnetized you—or me, at any rate; I read it, with the sense of charm that comes from the presence and touch of a delightful woman. Half the time I could not understand the sense of the passage I was perusing; but I did not care to understand it: I enjoyed it with some other faculty than the intellectual; it reached my heart without passing by way of the head.

Bettina, who has since become an historic figure, was a believer in the mysticism of words, and she would constantly use them without the least reference to their dictionary meaning. In the middle of the night, as she lay in bed thinking of her book, and of the means of conveying a sentiment or a perception, suddenly (she tells us) a word would pop into her head having just the sound and aspect that she needed, and she would jump up and write it down at once to make sure of it. There it stands in the text, having no more relation to the word logically required in that place than a dog's tail has to the zodiac.

You are simply to say it over and over to yourself until you get Bettina's feeling about it. (Perhaps this is where Gertrude Stein got her inspiration.) The end of it all was that the book became Bettina, and I doubt if I would know them apart if I were to see them together. There is a literary lesson in the story; there may turn out to be other ways of writing books than we conventionally imagine.

In the same category of extraordinary writers was Alfred Henry Lewis. It was not for nothing that Mr. Lewis occupied in journalism the high and unique position that he did. He possessed faculties that few men in the profession could rival. He could describe an occurrence or a scene; he could portray and analyze his character with a vividness and synthetic power that can hardly be surpassed.

Lewis feigned to have a philosophy to announce. He would talk to you of civilization and savagery, truth and lies, human nature, history and literature, sin and creation, God and protoplasm, foes and friends, or anything else that can engage the mind; on all of which he seemed to possess a vehement conviction, though in sober truth it may be doubted whether Lewis believed or disbelieved in anything. He was an imp of the perverse and a spinner of paradox. He would detect your weak point and cruelly dig you in it.

As for language, it existed for him, not he for it; he regarded it no more than a New York policeman regards a curate. If he were in need of a word or a phrase, the last place he looked for it was in his grammar or the dictionary. He created it on the spot, and left it to shift for itself—quite in the fashion of Bettina von Arnim. He was a humorist in the old sense—a man of humors and fancies, irresponsible, reckless, and haphazard. "I am writing this thing," he seems to say on every page, "and I write it to please myself. If you find no meaning in it, let it alone."

What Lewis wrote had a smell of its own, a face and figure peculiar to itself. A style of movement, a complexion, a voice and character like no other. The pages, as you turn them, cease to look like paper and print, and begin to seem human: as delightfully human as Lewis himself was, a strong character, fearless, lovable.

The Cakewalk at Atlantic City

CURIOSITY led me to that strange and exciting Atlantic City. I recall there was to be a "cakewalk" given by a troupe of gifted Negroes. As I was about to enter the hall, I saw a young colored nursemaid guarding a perambulator—she found a spot where she could look into the hall, but of course had to remain outside.

All the soul in her black body was wrapt upon the scene enacting within. The mystic power of heredity had awakened in her vague, uncomprehended memories of something which she had seen and taken part in, hundreds of years before, in the shadowy glades of the vast Central African primeval forest. Not that that particular girl, who was under twenty years old, was ever herself in Africa; but her ancestors had been, and they were now crowding into her mind and seeing through her eyes.

The dark mighty trees had taken the place, in her imagination, of the banks of seats surrounding the long oblong of polished dancing floor, filled with fashionable folk. Instead of the conventional band of stringed instruments which was discoursing decorous jazz music, her ears were filled with the maddening tom-toms, the shrill, shrieking pipes, the dissonant clamor of blocks of wood smitten together, and for the cool, perfunctory hand-clapping that punctuated the figures of the dance, she heard the delirious cries, the demoniac yells, the frantic howlings of scores of naked savages, capering, leaping, tossing arms and legs, twisting and writhing in the wild red glimmer of the blazing faggots. Of those savages she was one: how could she remember that she was nursemaid to a white baby?

But at the voice of her mistress who had returned from some errand, the spell of heredity was broken, and she sadly took up her black-woman's burden and her place was promptly filled.

But the dance went on, a dance for which we have invented comic names—cakewalk, jazz, and the like—but which, in its original form, was in full swing before America was heard of: and we ourselves in our Tuxedo coats were a savage horde of Goths and Vandals, swarming into eastern Europe.

The dance, a descendant from the ancient voodoo dance, is so masked as to excite our thoughtless amusement instead of our terror: it is no longer accompanied by unmentionable rites, and the mysterious powers of darkness are no longer evoked to work their ghastly spells; but the thing is at heart and in basic motive the same as it was in its untrammeled freedom a thousand years ago.

Of course that dance on the Steel Pier presented the very latest refinements which our culture has imposed upon the native orgy: there were ballet steps, as you could see in the opera, and the master of ceremonies was inexhaustible in his formal posings, his formal bows, etc. His suave authority continually checked the frenzy of the voodoo serpent when it was on the brink of breaking forth, and when the figure of the dance showed symptoms of transcending the smug bounds set down for it, he would shift it to another, and so avert the peril which he knew not of except beneath the surface of his consciousness.

But look at those marvelously wriggling flexible limbs, those up-tossing arms, those writhing bodies, those heads nodding so grotesquely, those quick bounds and abrupt haltings, those toadlike crouchings and hoppings, those jerky staccato advancings and retreatings, those fantastic starings and grimacings into one another's faces! All the time the rhythmic beat keeps on, the evolutions become swifter, freer, suppler! Have a care, Master of Ceremonies! That vision of the mid-forest glade is coming back again and in another moment we shall behold what none of us has dreamed of!

But we had no misgivings—a pretty girl in front of me giggled, and her escort remarked hopefully, "They'll have the real ragtime in a minute." "And where did the real ragtime come from?" I asked myself.

But I had seen dancing enough for one night, so I made my way out and saw the dark glossy rollers moulding along in smooth succession towards the beach. Only let those rollers roll a little higher and advance a little more powerfully, and where, tomorrow morning, would be Atlantic City? And would the cakewalk and jazz and its like vanish, too? No, they and their forebears would outlast Atlantic City and a good many other things of ours that now appear substantial enough.

A Visit to India During the
Plague of 1897

AMONG the keenest experiences of my life was my visit to India, during the plague, in 1897. The plague, coupled with famine, was particularly severe that year, and conscientious persons here in America were asking if England was doing her best to abate them. So I was commissioned by the *Cosmopolitan Magazine* to go over and report on conditions there.

These people of India have been going on for four thousand years, and in spite of claims to esoteric knowledge, and their Swamis and great personages, the Hindus are the most ignorant people in the world. Hottentots and Australian aborigines have a practical science of their own, and can take care of themselves; but the Hindus not only know nothing, but are paralyzed by prejudices—by belief in what is not. They have been ruled by many despots, but the supreme despot is Caste.

There are not fewer than five hundred thousand distinct castes in India—the enumeration is official and authentic. And members of one caste are precluded from free intercourse with those of any other. Physical contacts are forbidden—even spiritual ones, too, in some cases. I mustn't eat what you have touched, you mustn't sit on my chair, etc.; and the penalty for breaking this law is not material but post-mortem—eternal damnation of soul and body. As an illustration of this adherence to caste rules, I cite the following.

I was eating some bread and cheese, sitting the while on a bench outside a railway station in India; an American missionary sat beside me. Before us appeared a Hindu Brahman; they are distinguished by a bit of string round the neck. He was a moribund old skeleton, naked to the breech-clout, his feet cracked.

His sunken eyes rested on my lunch; his fleshless palms were brought together in supplication. But when I reached out my bread and cheese to him, he sadly recoiled from it as from poison. "What does he want then?" I asked the missionary. "Isn't he hungry?"

"He'll die of starvation tonight—his feet show it," was the reply; "but his caste won't let him take it from you."

We devised a plot—transparent, but it worked. I passed my lunch to the missionary; he went round the corner with it, and returned with it wrapped in paper. The Brahman accepted it and tottered off. "They don't mind us missionaries," my friend explained; "they regard us as more spirit than flesh, I suppose."

After landing in Bombay, I went afoot to see the town. The narrow streets were thronged with half-naked Hindus and turbaned Mohammedans, and every few moments a stretcher would pass along carrying a corpse: the plague was evidently hard at it. In fact, more than a million people were dying every day, and half of them by starvation. For the monsoon—as they call the rains—had failed that year, and there was no grain to eat. It was one of the big famines; and skeletons

—and a living skeleton is a queer sight—were stalking ghastly about the streets, and once in a while crumpling up and passing out then and there.

I joined General Gatacre and his squad of half a dozen young fellows and one native inspector, and we went into places which would make Tophet seem like an airy summer resort at the seaside. There was, for instance, a huge brick building, six stories high, enclosing an interior court—a native apartment-house. Rooms fifteen feet by eight opened out of corridors: each room contained a dozen to fifteen persons, sitting shoulder to shoulder on benches surrounding a long table; on the other side of the dark corridor was an opening for the throwing out of refuse! It fell to the bottom of the oblong court, which was never cleaned out, and in which, in the course of years, it had got packed solid with filth, twelve feet deep and more. From this festering mass arose a stench which was all the denizens had to breathe.

I dined at the English Club that evening, a pleasant place, on the Bay, punkahs sweeping backward and forward overhead, to stir up the dead air. They showed me a big glass cage, containing a live king cobra: a reptile twenty feet long, with a spread of hood as wide as a dinner plate; his bite had poison enough to kill a herd of oxen. They kill ten to twenty thousand every year, but mostly natives: as he reared up at me to a height of five feet, flickering his tongue, I was not sorry for the glass between us.

I spent a week in Bombay: in its fetid miasma of plague and famine. Never had I seen such a city before. There was the Bazaar—the native quarter, which is the real Bombay—narrow, crooked alleys, fantastic houses impending over them, ill-omened crevices between,

cavern-booths loaded with deep-hued stuffs and sparkling gems or metals, and a gray beard and gleaming
eyes on the watch, spider-like, within; yellow shafts of
sunlight alighting here and there on a Moslem turban
or a Hindu poll amid the silent, interweaving throngs
barefooting on the pavements, lean torsos, visages meager or bearded, sullen, vacant, cryptic behind their veil
of millenniums; and death-marks stamped on doorposts
by British inspectors—little white rings—where the
plague had been; and if a cross were added, a death.

Sometimes, on the floor above these street cavern-
shops, we caught glimpses through half-drawn curtains,
red or green—a moment's vision of an interior, of figures, grouped or single, faces in sharp light and shadow,
grotesque draperies, luminous against darkness, Arabian
Nights vistas, strange scents, everywhere brooding heat.

In daylight, we would wander through large spaces,
where uprose great mosques and temples and slender
minarets in honor of the dead gods. In the open air before a mosque, or within the wide arches, would often
kneel praying crowds of white-robed Moslems prostrat-
ing themselves before Allah.

Discarding pessimistic reflections as best I might, I
left the pestilent atmosphere of Bombay on a train for
Jubbulpore, the Taj Mahal, and way stations. There
was a bench on each side of the car covered with black
leather, slippery and smutty; the unglazed windows
were supplied with wooden jalousies, which kept out
the view but admitted everything else. The water in the
ice-water jar was hotter than any I would venture to
shave with; the car jolted like an old-fashioned coach on
the prairies of 1870.

The journey lasted from morning till evening across

the baked desert mud-flats, now and then crossing the bed of a river, its waterless course tracked over by footprints of human beings and animals. More interesting were the occasional desert trees, which drank their water from everlasting springs a hundred or more feet underground, and spread out far-extending branches, casting the only shade for barren leagues around. Under this shade were huddled human bodies, which had crept there for shelter on their endless and aimless treks from one abandoned village to another: there they squatted, all dead now, their flimsy garments fluttering around them, except when jackals had pulled the skeletons apart, in the hopeless search for marrow.

Jubbulpore at last—a big swarming city in the midst of the great Punjab peninsula. It was poignantly picturesque in the style of ten or twenty centuries ago. The famine had not visited Jubbulpore as yet; it was aside from the path of devastation. Meanwhile the citizens squatted indifferent, children of fate.

I carried letters of introduction to an American missionary who with his wife and family had sojourned in the wilderness for more than thirty years. The loveliest people I had ever seen were the converts he had made who came to his little white house in the afternoon. Their faces were beautiful in feature, and in expression full of the holiness of selfless love: their influence was like that of reading a chapter of the New Testament in faith and humility.

The son of the missionary became my guide the following day. We passed through the gateway of the deserted village. A few fleshless figures lurked here and there; but we came to a mud hut near the center of the enclosure. At first I thought it was empty. The furnishings were simple: a shelf three feet wide, and extending the length of the hut; I discerned something on the shelf. At first I took it for a heap of rubbish, but through the duskiness the dull glimmer of a pair of eyes met mine; the rubbish was a human figure, with a strip of ragged calico about the loins.

He began to mumble something, my guide interpreted: "He no longer believes in his own god, for it has not answered his prayers, for money enough for his funeral." This faithless god appeared in the form of a brown pebble, an oval irregular shape about five inches long. They were called lingams and were incarnations of Krishna, or of Siva. They had been brought to India from Egypt. This specimen was smooth, almost polished from the contact of myriads of praying hands, beseeching (I was told) the blessing of male children—and also good fortune in love affairs.

I asked if he would take a dollar for it—"He would die happy," my guide assured me. When the suggestion was made to the venerable skeleton, his eyes gleamed with a strange joy. That night he died.

A Quaker Family in Cambridge

NOT every Mountain came to Mahomet: sometimes we went to them, at least I did, having made friendships in the Concord-Cambridge neighborhoods during my college years—Ned Hallowell and his family for instance, who lived in Medford, not far from the Stearnses.

They were the darlings of mankind, at least of that part of Harvard mankind that was lucky enough to circumvent or to crash the gates, as they say now. Ned himself was a Philadelphia Quaker, among the last of a fading institution, but the scent of the roses clung to it still. We loved and respected him, and his charming little wife.

The more I meditate upon the period in New England when I was a college boy, the more incredibly innocent it looks; a sort of Golden Age time, in spite of the Civil War. Was it because what we fought for were generous principles, whereas the recent disturbance was stimulated by greed and terror? At any rate, the years from 1864 to 1914 didn't seem especially sinful or sinbreeding. And I can affirm that Ned Hallowell's circle, family and friends, were worth living with, and for.

There was always a group of college youth about the billiard table with "Ned" as we called him, ever ready for a game. But the arrival of the young ladies was the signal for us to be done with such trifles—and oh, such young ladies! young Quakeresses, fresh and fragrant, from Philadelphia, but of the newer generation, with the "Thee" left out, except among themselves, which rendered them all the more adorable. For to address a man as "you" had for them the kind of stimulating effect that we of today find (or expect) from a cocktail: it imparted I know not what emotion of kicking over the traces and adventuring into a rare spiritual freedom, like the maiden in the famous picture called "September Morn." Spiritual cocktails are infinitely more enkindling than whiskey ones, and the next-morning consequences are of tender dreams, not megrims. Are there such Quakeresses and such cocktails now?

"This—all this—was in the olden time, long ago."

Here, for a breathing-space, we draw rein, having passed through the valley of Boyhood, and come to the hills and mountains of Maturity and Age. But the journey had peculiar features.

Some young fellow recently published an autobiographical volume, which he called "The First Twenty Years." A courageous title, I thought. What of his eighty-fifth year—if he should come to that? The world and he would have had their vicissitudes. Would he have carried on the record unbroken, or would he have chosen to delete some of it—or would he deem it the better part of wisdom to chuck the whole bundle of dog-eared manuscript into the fire, and sit staring into the grate, in his study easy-chair, with the light of the flames flickering over his white hair, and reflected from his meditative spectacles!

The three hundred or so pages which now lie on my desk, however, have a sounder claim to existence than as portraying my own beginnings, and mature recollections. But it happened that I drew my first breath in the atmosphere of a famous period here in New England, and inadvertently, and myself invisible, saw and noted my environment. And Time, which takes away so much, had given unique value to these snap-shots, because, like the man in "ob" I alone am escaped to tell thee! No other person still alive shared my good fortune or could duplicate my story. My father was one of the elect, and caused me to become a sort of household intimate of those friends of his. They were my daily companions, whom I remember all the better, perhaps, because I didn't know that they were particularly worth remembering. Of a thousand episodes I set down not what was intrinsically important, but what I happened, personally, to recall. If, rambling about Stratford-on-Avon, you chanced upon an old shoe, discarded three centuries ago by William Shakespeare, you would prize it, and it would help you to understand his plays and sonnets.

But if, at the time, I didn't fully appreciate my luck, there was more of it to come; though the tall men I looked up to are gone, others, my own contemporaries, have succeeded them. And though, had I held to my first intention, of becoming a civil engineer, I might have built Brooklyn Bridge, the profession into which I fell (against my father's warning) has brought me acquaintances with many of the men and women best worth knowing in the world.